HOME
IS WHERE I LAY MY HEAD DOWN

Walking Across America

HOME

IS WHERE I LAY MY HEAD DOWN

Walking Across America

Kent Treptow

Edited By Alicia Robinson

First printing 2014

ISBN:978-1-312—19478-6

Photographs and illustrations by the author.

Published by Kent Treptow
Newport Beach, CA
kent.treptow@gmail.com

www.kenttreptow.com

For my parents

Wells Beach, Maine

Even in June the ocean in Maine is black, the sky a little less so. Gray swell and whitewater blur the line between the two. Rain ripples on pools where hermit crabs hide in seaweed green and slippery. Waves are running sideways down the beach, driven by the wind.

I've always had three great fears in life — sharks, cockroaches and beautiful women. Sharks, because I've grown accustomed to being fat and happy atop the food chain, and don't like being bumped to middle-of-the-road entrée whenever I dip my toes in the water. Cockroaches, because I once read a story in the *National Enquirer* about a village in the Amazon that was wiped out when invading roaches crawled up everyone's noses at night, thereby suffocating them. And beautiful women? Well, because they're beautiful, and I'm not.

But now, standing on this gray and dismal beach thousands of miles from home, a new fear arises. A fear of uncertainty, of not knowing. A fear of being vulnerable all the time. And this fear will not come and go. It will be with me every day, when I ask myself if I'm strong enough, brave enough. When I wonder where I'm going to sleep every night. And when I hear the question asked every day by waitresses in back-road diners, by ranchers, convenience store clerks, highway patrolmen and Amish farmers, by truckers, cowboys, Indians, tourists, drunks and drug addicts, and by myself whenever I'm cold or wet or hungry or frightened:

What am I doing?

I have no idea.

Rain drumming on my backpack. Smell of the ocean one last time. My brother waves from the car with the engine running. I turn and walk away.

What was that thing you always wanted to do, always wanted to be? A race car driver? A rock star? An astronaut? For me, it was treasure hunter. I was going to roam the Caribbean in a converted fishing trawler hunting sunken treasure, corroded gold crucifix around my neck from the Spanish galleon I'd just found. Second choice was globe-trotting photographer. That's what I settled on.

Just as the race car driver now pilots a cement mixer and the astronaut sells health insurance, I ended up at a newspaper 10 miles from where I grew up. What was supposed to be a first step, then on to bigger things, turned into years of trying to climb a ladder whose rungs had rotted away. Stuck. Sleepwalking. Piling up regrets. I rode that horse into the ground. And when it dropped I stood over it, kicking, prodding and pleading for it to get back up. And then I let it go.

One year ago, south of Escondido, California

"Yer doin' what now?" the man asks through a gap-toothed smile, wad of tobacco under his lip, eyes half-hidden under the brim of a filthy black cowboy hat.

"Walking across the country."

"Ha! I bet you are!" he laughs back, slapping the door of his rusty pickup through the open window.

"Are ya drunk?"

"Nope."

"Crazy?"

"A little."

"Stupid?"

"Definitely."

He laughs again, shakes his head and rolls up his window. I watch him go. A few hours later my first attempt at this walk will be over almost before it begins, on Day Three, in a flash of headlights and crunching metal as the cart I'm pulling is shattered by a passing car. The driver never stops, but that's a footnote; this is a disaster of my own making. Walking on a mountain road, at night, with a dog I barely know. The dumbest thing I've ever done.

Hanna's leash gets wrapped around one of the cart's axles and we're forced to stop on a blind corner. Two cars round the bend at 60 miles an hour only to find a derelict hobo and his scraggly mutt dead ahead, off to the right but in line with their tires because the drivers have cut the corner, like everyone does, because they're in a hurry, and they're tired and they want to get home and no one would ever be stupid enough to walk here and oh my God what the hell is that NO! A split-second to react, hit him or swerve into oncoming traffic? The first car misses, the second one connects, with a sound like a baseball bat hitting an aluminum trash can. Four more inches and we're dead. But the stupidity that placed us here has also saved us, because in order to untangle the leash, neither of us is attached to the cart, as we would have been at any other time. And that's the difference. Not even a scratch. But the cart is gone, and so is my courage, my will. This walk is over.

I head home. Apart from a few "I told you so" looks, everyone is supportive. But I've failed myself. A year of planning to have it fall apart during the first week. I tell people it's too dangerous to try again with a cart, even though I need one to haul my water and food across those big, empty, lonely deserts. But the truth is, I'm afraid. Afraid of almost dying the first time. Afraid that I'm not tough enough, that I'm too much of a dreamer.

I move back in with my maybe girlfriend. I say "maybe" because I'm not really sure if she still is — maybe, maybe not. It's a risk you run when you suddenly announce that you're leaving your life, everything, her included, and disappearing for six months. But she just smiles and welcomes me back.

I drift for a couple of months, making half-hearted attempts to fit into real jobs. I work on my resume, write some cover letters. They all begin the same way:

Dear Evil Corporate Bastard,

I am writing to express my interest in the position of faceless drone/expendable working stiff for (insert company name here) . . .

I fill out applications. Make phone calls. Get nowhere. I'm starting to think that quitting my job in the middle of a recession wasn't the best idea. Then, as luck would have it, a spot opens at my old newspaper again. My photo editor has quit for the same unhappy reasons I did. So I take his place, comfortable, safe and secure. A bird come home to the cage.

This second stint lasts all of six months. That thing that sabotaged me in the first place — the one that doesn't pay attention to logic, won't listen to reason, isn't fazed by circumstances — it gnaws at me. For a long time now I've been trapped. I know what that's like. I just don't know how to settle.

So for the second time in a year I march into the editor's office and hand in my resignation.

"You sure you want to do this?"

"I'm sure."

Down the hallway, past the fountain that's broken or was turned off to save money, don't know which, out the glass doors, past the guard shack. Walking away from what was supposed to be my dream job, the thing I was going to do, happily, for the rest of my life.

This time I will be alone. Hanna is frolicking with a pair of Australian shepherds on a ranch north of San Diego. Hanna was my greeting card, the goofy ambassador with one floppy ear who made people look twice and not instantly dismiss me as a hobo, which I am, or a serial killer, which I am not. She was my guardian while sleeping in unfamiliar places. She was the friend I would speak to on cold, lonely nights.

But Hanna would never have made it. I knew it long before I found her at the county shelter, the last stop before the needle and the fire and the burial at sea, the place so overflowing with desperate and discarded animals that few questions are asked when someone shows up to offer one a new life, even if the first six months of that life will be spent on the open road. She is my third choice, after the brown and white husky, and a chocolate lab mix. The husky turns out to be a bucking bronco that chases after every squirrel, bird and housefly that buzzes by its nose, and the lab just lies down every ten feet and refuses to get up. Someone suggests a Chihuahua, and there certainly is no shortage of those. Eighty percent of the dogs at the shelter are Chihuahuas. Why?

"Movie stars," the shelter volunteer tells me. "They carry these things with them wherever they go," he says, waving his hand at an entire row of yapping, bouncing little dogs.

"Like a handbag with ears."

"Yup, just like that. A handbag. People see them on T.V. and they want one just like it. But then they pee on the carpet or people get bored with them, and they end up here."

And how is a dog that's half the size of a cat going to walk across America?

I round the corner and wander down the second row, past more Chihuahuas and a couple of empty pens. At the third cage from the end, I see a motionless lump of white and black fur bulging from the concrete at the far end of the enclosure. The tag on the front says Australian shepherd mix, followed by a question mark. Picked up as a stray. As I kneel down a single ear sticks up at the end of the lump, a prelude to her now familiar, one-ear-up-one-down charm offensive that reduces both children and adults to fawning mushballs elbowing each other out of the way for petting rights. I tap on the cage and a tail materializes, gently slapping the cement floor. She gets to her feet and wanders over, resting her head on the bars, sniffing my hand. Then she picks up a toy to play tug-of-war. Keep your head, man, don't be fooled by cute mannerisms and a bit of hand licking. A quick check reveals some deep cuts and bloody spots with no hair on them. But then she rests her head on my hand, gently pinning it to the floor. Damn. I'm falling for it.

The vet checks her out, says he thinks she got rolled under a car, but seems to have no internal problems or broken bones. There's no limping. We take a few short walks, in which she strides directly off my left leg (the perfect spot if you're walking against traffic) while glancing up at me every few seconds, as if to say, "Is this okay? Am I doing okay, dad?" I'm sold.

But like most things that seem too good to be true, such is the case with Hanna. I live in an apartment with no yard, so Hanna goes to stay with my friend Susan while we train. It's a great place for her, a yard she can destroy on a daily basis, and two canine friends, Bennie and Angel, to play with. But here is the first problem. Despite several months of twice daily training, walking and running at least four miles in the morning and the same amount at night, we never live together. We don't bond the way we should, and I feel more like a really good friend to someone else's dog instead of its owner. And as much as I pretend to be a dog whisperer — "I am the pack leader," I say over and over — she slowly starts to assert herself, to our detriment.

Whereas in the beginning she ran directly off my hip, now she begins to stray, a habit that gets worse until it culminates in a trip to the veterinary ER after she chases a seagull into a lifeguard tower at the beach and shreds her legs while jumping around the metal support beams. Ten stitches in her front leg, 10 staples in the back and a month wearing the cone of shame on her head that makes her look like a 1960s lampshade. Cost? A thousand dollars.

I did a lot of research before attempting this journey. Read a lot of blogs. A good number start out the same way — someone hates his or her job, quits said job and hits the road with nothing but a backpack and a loyal, loveable mutt. He or she is going to write a book (aren't we all?). But most of these blogs end suddenly after a week or two, when it becomes apparent that walking across the country with a dog is a whole lot harder than you think it's going to be. The extra food and water weight alone is enough to sink it, then imagine your dog being rushed by other dogs, or suddenly veering into traffic to chase a bird, or getting her nose into a porcupine or rattlesnake or scorpion, or barking in the middle of the night when you're trying to keep quiet, because you're camping where you're not supposed to. Or maybe when it gets hot she just decides she's not going to walk. She gets destroyed by ticks. Cuts her paws. The list goes on.

So the warning signs are there. I choose to ignore them. I am going to make this work, there's no stopping us. If I paid attention to all the "what ifs" I'd never leave the couch. Sheer determination will see us through.

Goodbye Hanna. I miss you.

MAINE

NEW HAMPSHIRE

VERMONT

Highway 9 leaves the coast of Maine and weaves through marshes and waving grasses, mud bogs thick as molasses. Past summer homes of rich people from New York and Boston, through open wetlands into scattered stands of trees. Within minutes these forest islands have closed in behind me, leafy blinds pulled tight in a solid wall of trees that blocks out the sea. I can smell the ocean. I can hear it. But I won't see it again for six months.

I make only 17 miles, but that's because I start at noon and take a couple of wrong turns along the way. Two days ago it was 96 degrees. Now it's 49 and raining. I've been walking in my rain parka, a huge blue thing that covers not only me but my backpack as well, making me look like a walking trash bag or an Easter egg on the lam from some kid's collection basket. What's worse, the color bleeds with the moisture, so that when I take it off I look like the lost 5th member of the Blue Man Group. "Don't mind me, on my way to Vegas for a drum circle . . ."

I set up camp beside a forest stream as the summer sun sets. Check my watch: 8:30 p.m.. I'm still alive. I haven't cried, or been mugged or shot, as several people assured me I would be. I find a mushroom that vaguely resembles the Virgin Mary, which I take as a good sign despite the fact that I'm not the least bit religious.

I tie up my food in a tree because I'm bored and it makes me feel like a man, though I have no idea if there are bears in this forest or just mice and raccoons. The rain stops before midnight, replaced by a creeping mist that swirls in shafts of moonlight filtering through the trees. I watch it until I see ghosts, then retreat to the safety of my tent, wondering if it's ghost-proof, hoping the mushroom will protect me. Day One has ended.

Even without Hanna, dogs are a concern. I'm usually quite good with them, as I am with small children, which I take as a sign of my good character. You can't fool dogs and babies; they see right through you. But these country dogs are hard to read. I never know what I'm getting — angry watchdog, herding dog or beloved family pet? Nearly every farmhouse has some sort of bored mutt rolling in the dirt, eating flies and mosquitoes when they feel like it, lazily following them with their eyes when they don't. I start playing a game invented while traveling through various third-world places with my friend Tom, a game called "Dead or Sleeping?" in which you try to guess whether the creature in question has indeed expired or is simply comatose from boredom, heat or eating too many squirrels. These particular dogs generally ignore all the usual distractions you'd find on a farm — sheep, cattle, birds eating kibble from their food bowls, groundhogs shuffling beneath the steps of the house — but have a guy walk by with a backpack and they act like there's a parade of baton-twirling cats in bacon vests marching down the highway. So they go from "Dead or Sleeping?" to killing machine in 1.6 seconds, regardless of size. Even the ones I could punt across the yard like a football.

Still in Maine, just outside Dover, I get rushed by a pit bull. A tattooed guy with a mohawk follows. I prepare to defend myself but all the dog really wants to do is chase its tail in the middle of the highway, which it does, as the man tries to pull it off the road. Traffic stops and begins backing up. This goes on for awhile until an enormous lady in a floral muumuu appears in the doorway of the house, clutching a 40-ounce bottle of something despite the fact that it's 8:15 in the morning. She takes a swig and begins screaming profanities at man and beast, mostly man. Mohawk runs back to the house, where the enormous lady promptly grabs him by the hair and throws him inside, slamming the door behind her. Dog keeps running in circles on the road as motorists honk their horns and scream at it to no avail.

I begin my trek into New Hampshire. One state down, 14 to go. I have crossed Maine in one day, which sounds impressive until one realizes I only had 15 miles of it to cross. Why start in Maine? Because New York to Los Angeles just sounded too easy. I needed something so big I couldn't see across it, a test of everything, on all levels — physical, mental, emotional. New York to L.A.? Too pedestrian. But Maine to L.A.? Just right. Walking across America, the longest way across America — across a country, a continent, the space between two oceans.

In Keene it won't stop raining, so I take shelter on the porch of a closed tax preparation office. A police car speeds by then suddenly screeches to a halt. It reverses and peels into the parking lot. Great. Going to get arrested for loitering my first week.

This will be the fourth time in my life I get arrested, which will come as a shock to my mother. Once it was for public intoxication and twice for espionage. But I was innocent of all charges. I swear. The first time was in a Mexican border town, a shakedown by corrupt cops who knew an opportunity when they saw one — a trio of idiot American teenagers standing on a sidewalk, one with a red plastic cup of beer in his hand. That's a gimme. An afternoon in a holding cell followed, a delightful few hours spent sloshing sneaker-deep in an opaque mystery liquid on the floor while a group of drunken Mexican street thugs took turns whispering, "I'm going to keel jew!" from the next cell over. A visit from my friend's dad and a fistful of $20 bills sprung us from that one.

My second run-in with the law occurred at a border crossing in central Africa, when a soldier eager to pad his beer-and-prostitutes account pulled me out of line to accuse me of "spying." Some flimsy thing about a visa with a forged signature, which was actually fairly enterprising since they usually just said "Give me money" or went through your bag and took whatever they wanted. When he got up to use the toilet — he seemed to be hooked on chai tea or coffee, maybe both — a minibus pulled up to the wide-open front door and the smiling man in the driver's seat motioned for me to get in. So I grabbed my bag, sprinted out the door and did just that. And that's how you turn a $50 get-out-of-jail fee into a $4 taxi fare to the next border crossing.

I had a final slip-up in Mongolia, where I was photographing a story. As I was sitting in the airport taking a picture of my interpreter, Tselmeg, an unsmiling airport security guard in a military-green, suit jacket-and-miniskirt combination walked up to hiss and wag her finger at us. Apparently I was compromising airport security with my camera. Since there were a half-dozen other western tourists sitting in the lobby also snapping pictures of themselves, Tselmeg didn't see a problem and told her to go screw herself. She promptly disappeared in a huff and returned a short time later with two equally humorless Cold War types who then led us away for interrogation.

In a dimly lighted underground room I was passed off to a chain-smoking fat man who sat behind a desk and listlessly thumbed through my passport, saying things like, "This looks very bad for you" while I alternated between looking appropriately concerned and trying not to burst out laughing. After 45 minutes of this nonsense there was a knock at the door and a man entered holding a cell phone at arm's length, as if it were about to explode. My interrogator took the phone and stepped outside while the other guy lit up a cigarette and took his place glaring sternly at me. A minute later the fat man returned. But something was different — he was smiling. He handed me a steaming cup of coffee and began apologizing for any inconvenience, patting me on the back and calling me his "friend" over and over. What was going on?

My interpreter appeared moments later, also smiling. It turned out that Tselmeg, in addition to being an interpreter, also happened to be the son of the chief of security for the president of Mongolia. Very convenient.

"You called your dad, didn't you?" I asked.

He just smiled again.

And soon everyone was smiling, even the security lady who started the whole thing, though the effort made her look like her jaw might break off.

Thus ended my life of crime. I've been clean ever since. Until now.

The Concord police officer approaches cautiously, telling me to have a seat on the curb. I still don't understand, guessing there was a rash of burglaries in the area and I fit the description — "Caucasian. Dirty. Looks homeless." After he runs my I.D. I ask him what's going on and he says "We don't see people like you around here much." But he turns out to be courteous and helpful after determining I'm not really breaking into a tax preparation office, and offers to drive me to the edge of town. I'm still not sure if it's a sincere offer to help or an attempt to kick me down the road to become someone else's problem. But when I decline his offer he just smiles and tells me to have a nice day.

Summer in New England is buggy. I've missed the black flies by a couple of weeks, but the ants, mosquitoes, spiders, and houseflies are filling in nicely. The ticks are the worst. I've begun referring to them simply as "The Enemy" because their attack is merciless and methodical, and they never stop coming. Any foray into the grass off the side of the road yields three or four of them on my shoes, soon up to my ankles, past my socks and on to juicier, more tender places. If I don't perform a check every five minutes I'm guaranteed a dozen of them up my thighs —or much worse — by lunch time. And they don't die.

Execution by slapping, pinching, smashing or squishing is nearly impossible. I try knocking them to the ground and stomping them beneath my shoes. They just keep going, grinding away like little tanks. Nights are a horror show of tiny silhouettes crawling up the outside of the tent, patiently looking for a way in.

At the Friendly's restaurant in Keene I meet an enemy of a different sort. Friendly's is like an East Coast version of Denny's, only instead of Moons over My Hammy they serve things like the Lumberjack and the Super Sizzler. It's cheap and greasy, and the waitress calls me "honey." In the booth behind me a young boy is going ballistic, screaming at his parents and kicking the table, causing the dishes to clatter and rattle violently across it. When his father speaks the kid just screams over him, and when his mother tries he tells her to shut up. He's about four years old.

After several minutes of nonstop tantrums an old man in overalls and a baseball cap gets up from across the aisle and ambles over to their table.

"Just want you to know you ruined our breakfast," he says.

"What?" says the father, feigning surprise and indignation.

"Your boy's bad manners ruined our breakfast and probably ruined everyone else's too."

The father rises out of the booth and looks wildly around the restaurant, daring anyone to agree with the old man. So I do, by raising my hand. He glares at me.

"I thought this was a public restaurant!" he says, voice rising. "I thought this was America!"

The old man starts to say something but the father yells over him, like his boy does to him, stepping toward the old-timer in a threatening manner. The old man shakes his head, takes his wife by the arm and shuffles out the door.

"This is America!" the father yells after him. And it won't be the last time I hear those words.

He sits back down and starts mumbling about his "rights," just loud enough for the entire restaurant to hear. Whenever his crummy kid looks up at me I smile, with an open mouthful of food, and his crummy kid smiles right back.

I walk through the town of Brattleboro and a skunk is walking in circles in the road, lowering its head like a bull facing down a matador, spinning and raising its tail every time a car inches up to it. Another major traffic jam. A group of college students is hanging out on a porch watching, so I try to strike up a conversation. They just ignore me, the first of many, probably assuming I'm homeless. So instead of sleeping on a couch with pretty co-eds I'm off into the forest dodging The Enemy for another night. I find a small island in a beaver pond and make camp on it, kicking away the stepping stones once I'm across, pulling up the drawbridge for the night. Water reflects the clouds and surrounding trees, its perfect glass broken only by resident beavers slapping their tails on the far shore. Lightning bugs blink at the edge of the forest, hundreds of them, drifting like candles held by wandering spirits. I cup one in my hands; its light glows between my fingers. Gunshots echo across the ridgelines, very far away. I skinny dip with the last light of the day.

I have never been to New England. I never appreciated the beauty of it, thinking it had to fall short of the dramatic deserts and mountains in the West. But now I see it up close, and it's gorgeous. Daisies bloom around old stone churches, broken tombstones half hidden by tufts of waving grass. Leaning red barns slowly collapse into sodden meadows filled with purple irises. People mow their lawns and it looks like they're cutting down fields of wildflowers. They just call them weeds.

The forest is endless, the wildlife prolific. I hear or see deer everywhere — walking down the middle of the road, wading in rivers, nibbling potted plants in someone's yard or snapping twigs outside my tent at night. Down the road I will even see them placidly grazing on the shooting range of the Gowanda Rifle Club, like targets, as if saying, "Shoot me first! No, me! I want to be shot first!" Apart from the aforementioned noisy beavers, I've seen turtles, hawks, eagles, wild turkeys, a bear and possibly Sasquatch. There are road signs warning of "moose crossings" though I haven't seen one crossing yet.

There are some unwelcome visitors as well. The morning after my skinny dip, I get up to take a leak and something feels a bit off. I make a quick inventory of my private parts. Okay, there's one of those, and two of those. But what's that other thing dangling there?

Oh . . . my . . . God.

It's a leech.

Some things are beyond words. Some things a man takes with him to the grave. So I'll spare the gory details. Suffice to say that when a leech is fat and happy it comes off rather easily. I pick it up, swollen and squishable, and wrap it in a quadruple layer of toilet paper. Just as I'm ready to send it back to God, or to hell, or wherever it is that it came from, I pause and reconsider. You know what? It took some doing to crawl all the way up in there. Some finesse, if you will. That leech is just doing what it does, and it's doing it well. My fault really for dangling my juicy bits above its lair and daring it not to attack. Don't swim with the sharks if you don't want to get bitten. And it's not like he just ate at Del Taco. This was a meal for the ages. He earned it. I unwrap him and flick him into the river to suck another day. God is merciful.

At a scenic overlook on Hogback Mountain, five college girls in tight denim shorts, tank tops — also very tight — and cowboy hats ask me to take their picture. I'm calling them college girls for legal reasons but they're freshmen at best. Possibly a stripping academy on a field trip.

"Okay, on three. One . . . two . . . three . . ."

At three they scream "Woo-hoo!", and the tank tops go up, all the way up. Giggles and more screaming. They say thanks, and without thinking I thank them right back.

A couple days later in a town whose name I can't remember, a stoned kid in a Chevy Blazer slows to a crawl on the opposite side of the street and sticks his head out the window.

"Holy shit, bro! What're you doing?"

"Walking across America."

"Holy shit!"

He rolls along on the far side of the road for ten minutes, matching my pace, yelling questions and encouragement across traffic while driving over discarded beer bottles in the gutter and backing up traffic for a hundred yards behind him.

"You alone, bro?"

"Yeah."

"Walking the whole way, bro?"

"Yeah."

"Holy sh . . . !"

Horns honk and people start yelling. He doesn't notice.

"Smoke weed, bro?"

"No."

That one throws him a bit, like he just got asked an algebra question in remedial math class. He can't quite fathom it.

"Holy shit . . ." he stammers. "Bro . . . you gotta start!"

Drivers are really getting agitated. One of them peels out into oncoming traffic to pass, and my friend finally takes note. Screaming "Peace out!" he crumples a $5 bill in his hand and chucks it out the window, where it promptly gets run over by a semi and several SUVs. He drives off with his fist in the air. Two minutes later I can safely cross the highway to claim my five bucks, crumpled into blackened origami by rush hour traffic.

At a country diner the conversation stops as I come in, as if a gunslinger just walked through the door and people are weighing whether to draw their weapons or dive for cover. Everyone looks like a logger, even the women. Lots of plaid and denim. A sign above the grill says "COUNTRY GIRLS RULE!" On the counter, a large plastic jar full of dollar bills has a picture of a woman about to pull up her top, saying, "SHOW ME YOUR TIPS!"

I sidle up to a stool to order a Diet Pepsi — instead of whiskey — and the conversation starts where it left off. The guy next to me asks what I'm doing, inevitably followed by "You got a gun?" and "Are you an idiot?"

"Nah, don't carry a gun," I say. "But I wrestle bears for a living and can kill a tick just by staring at it. Might be an idiot. The jury's out."

Silence, several seconds of it. Then someone a few stools down chuckles, and soon everyone is laughing. Thank you God, because until then I thought they might kill me. A stooped old man in the corner asks, "You wanna take my old lady with you?" She's sitting right beside him. More laughter. People gather around. It takes me two hours to eat my ham and cheese omelet. When I'm finished I go to pay my bill but the waitress tells me someone already did, a man at the end of the counter who left an hour ago and never said a word to me.

The highway is a killing field. Smashed turtles litter the asphalt, shells scattered like broken pottery, along with mysterious rotten blobs that could be either mangled animal

carcasses or discarded pepperoni pizzas. A new game —
"Name that Corpse" — replaces "Dead or Sleeping?" as I trip
over these ambiguous lumps and try to guess their identities.
Dog? Woodchuck? Calzone? And my first East Coast coyote,
the largest coyote I've ever seen. People claim there's a hybrid
in New England that's a mix of coyote and wolf, that it's much
larger and more dangerous than the coyotes out West. Say they
eat babies. Probably an urban legend, but I wouldn't test it by
leaving a baby out overnight on the front lawn.

This road deals out more than death. Every conceivable
object man could lose or chuck out of a vehicle lies in varying
states of demolition on the side of the road. Along with the
expected — hubcaps, mufflers, side-view mirrors, Big Gulps,
cell phones, and McDonald's french fry containers — are
televisions, computers, microwave ovens, pots, pans, knives, a
broken gun (yes, really), sofas, entire dining room sets, Barbie
dolls (usually just heads), iPods, American flags, snakeskin
boots, toy guitars, music CDs (Meat Loaf's "Bat Out of Hell"
still popular here) and an alarmingly complete selection of beer,
wine, whiskey and vodka bottles. A couple of empty wallets.
There's apparently a lot more than driving going on, as the
collection of bras, men's and women's underwear, dirty
magazines, condoms and "marital aids" (two of them so far)
would indicate. Oh, and people really seem to hate pennies. Or
they just hate Abraham Lincoln.

I find a dead SpongeBob SquarePants doll and consider
taking it along as a mascot, since I don't yet have imaginary
friends and it would be nice to have some company. Tom Hanks

had a volleyball ("Wilson" in *Castaway*), I'd have Bob. Then I realize it's probably a trick of The Enemy, like a Trojan SpongeBob, in which thousands of the little tick bastards come streaming out as soon as I strap it onto my pack. So I kick him square in his buck-toothed face to see what happens. Nothing. Then I kick him again because I feel like it.

The Appalachians end in a long downhill in western Vermont. The scenery changes at the New York border, thick canopy of trees replaced by farmland and isolated remnants of forest. Albany is my first big city. I hate big cities. Camping has been easy so far — just ditch off the road into the forest, find a stream and fall asleep to the lullaby of running water. Then farms appear, along with barbed wire fences that will not go away for 2,500 miles. Camping becomes more difficult. In cities it's impossible, unless I crawl behind a dumpster or under a bridge.

Being on the road is tiring. So tiring, in fact, that social filters erode and I find myself operating mostly by instinct and primal need alone, with little thought for pleasantries or manners. For example, two weeks ago I might have entered a bakery and politely asked for a couple of apple fritters and a cup of orange juice, and could you point me to the restroom, please? Now I'm as likely to blurt out "Want donuts!" or "Toilet!" in my best caveman voice.

Sometimes this is a good thing, I get what I want with a minimal expenditure of energy. And sometimes it's bad. Some filters are good for your health, and exist to keep you from getting punched in the face. One of these involves the three-second rule. Not to be confused with the more familiar "five-second rule," which states that dropped food is still safe to eat if plucked off the ground and popped in one's mouth within five seconds (regardless of how filthy that ground may be), the three-second rule postulates that when looking at a beautiful woman, anything less than three seconds falls into the category of "approving glance," while anything beyond that is considering leering, and labels you a pervert.

So, the three-second rule is usually the first to go. I see something I like, and I like to look at it. For a long time. Three seconds stretches to four, then to five. This is dangerous territory. It's like getting pulled over for drunk driving with a blood-alcohol level of .21 instead of .08. You're not just drunk, you're hammered. And when you're breaking the three-second rule by two or more seconds, you're risking rebuttal through slaps to the face, angry boyfriends or calls to the police.

Thus I find myself walking into Albany. Past a wooden gate I look up to see a beautifully restored farmhouse with a long, winding driveway. A woman in a hot pink slip and nothing else is walking barefoot down the drive. She's got about one extra inch on that slip before it becomes indecent, at least in the eyes of the law. Stopping at the mailbox, she stretches like a cat, does a little wiggle and leans over to check her mail. One, two, three . . . four, five . . . uh-oh. Just a few minutes ago at the mini-mart I busted myself for looking at the girl in the Coors Light ad a little too long. Now I walk into a telephone pole. But I'm looking at the part of her that doesn't look back, so my staring goes unnoticed. She grabs her mail, wiggles a bit more and strolls back up the drive. Six, seven, eight . . .

NEW YORK

In Albany I get lucky, as a last-second phone call connects me with Patrick, a friend of a friend willing to put me up for a couple of nights. I sit on the curb at the corner of Hoosick and 9th. Another man is already there, with a smile on his face and two teeth in his head. Never got his name, but he's from Guyana in South America. Tells me he has 13 children by five different women.

"When I die, mon, I want to come back as sweet soap!"

"You want to come back as soap?"

"Yeah mon, dat way I can caress all de ladies and melt on dey bodies!"

"Cool. Me, I want to come back as a dolphin."

"Ha! Dat boring, mon!"

He's still laughing when Patrick drives up.

I've been on the road for ten days, and Albany affords me my first day off. These rest days are necessary. I walk 20 to 30 miles a day, sometimes more, with a pack that varies from 35-50 pounds, depending on how much water and food I carry. That's a light pack, but it's still tough. Walking on pavement is unforgiving; I don't realize how much so until I've done it all day, every day, for a couple of weeks. There's no give in it, no cushion, and when the shoes start to fail, as mine are now, the body takes a beating. Add the sun, the heat, and the rain, and it's brutal.

But the greatest difficulty is not physical. Surprisingly for me, a person who likes having solo adventures and doing things by himself, the loneliness is the hardest part. I've been away from home many times, in far-flung places where I can't speak the language and all I am to most locals is a walking dollar sign. I never felt lonely. Here I do. It's that vulnerability, that uncertainty. I told myself this walk would make me unbreakable, that it would make me fearless. But the truth is you can't walk away. Your demons follow you. Wherever you go, there you are.

So I baby myself for a day. Initially I'm a bit wary as Patrick brings me home. His parents are away for the weekend, and with his 19-year-old brother, Alex, and a few friends in the house, I'm expecting togas, beer bongs and bonfires, with me playing the part of suspected undercover cop or, at the very least, the old guy who makes everyone else uncomfortable. But Patrick is tired from his work week. The closest thing to mayhem occurs during an animated game of Yu-Gi-Oh! (nerdy Japanese card game) when Alex's friend Eric takes a beating, so to speak, and yells:

"Did you see that! He combined Heavy Storm with Lightning Vortex! He destroyed my entire field!"

I have no idea what that means and I'm proud to say it. One of the kids gives me a card for the road as a gift: Red-Eyes Black Metal Dragon. I will carry it always to ward off evil. Will it ward off big rigs?

I leave Albany on a gray morning. It's cold and windy. Leaves scatter like startled birds. It starts raining, so I sit under a bridge like a transient for two hours waiting for it to stop. It never does. I slip into my rain parka, which I've named Blue Hefty because of its aforementioned resemblance to a giant trash bag. I slog through the city, just making the outskirts by nightfall.

Farms everywhere, nowhere to camp unnoticed. At these times I'm forced to approach a farmhouse to ask if I can pitch a tent on the far edge of their field somewhere. I look for homes with ceramic garden gnomes out front, which for some reason I associate with hospitality, or promising door mats that say things like "Welcome Friends!," or "Come on in!" I always make sure it's a big farm with a distant field so the owners don't feel like the strange man is asking to camp in the flower beds beneath the bedroom window. Most people say yes. Sometimes it's come in and make yourself comfortable, sometimes it's yes with reservations and occasionally it's no. Several people act like they can't hear the knock on the door, even when I can plainly see them sitting in the living room. Probably think I'm a Jehovah's Witness. One time a guy on his sofa turns around to look at me as I knock, so I wave to him and he just turns back to the T.V. I guess I do look homeless. This becomes evident one day when a small boy runs up to me in a park and yells "Hey, scavenger butt!" I give him a good whuppin' and send him home to his pappy. No, not really. But the backpack does make people wary.

This walk could be defined as "budget," which means I try to not pay for things as much as possible. Sometimes this gets me into trouble, like it nearly did in East Springfield. I realize it's probably not a good idea to visit a motel and ask the owner if I can sleep on the grass instead of paying for a room, but this is exactly what I do at the Otsego Motel. I walk in, he smiles. When I tell him I don't actually want a room, the smile leaves his face. I start mumbling.

"Well, I, um, I'm walking across the country."

"Congratulations," he deadpans, unimpressed and not amused. He looks like he's sizing up a con man while reaching under the table for his shotgun.

"I can pay you," I say promisingly. Still unimpressed. Without a word he leans toward the phone, probably to summon the townsfolk to gather up the torches and pitchforks and get down here quick. I start babbling.

"Well, uh . . . I'm, umm . . . I'm from California — "

He looks up. The frown leaves his face.

"California? Hey! I'm from California!"

Turns out he's a West Coast refugee who fled the big city to buy a ramshackle motel in the middle of nowhere. Just him and his wife, working for years to clear the field out front and renovate the buildings. The only thing they leave untouched is the vintage 60-year-old sign.

He's laughing now. Sure I can camp. Anywhere. Heck, it might rain tonight, take the house. Not his house. The other house, which now becomes *my* house. He sets me up in a detached two-storey out the back, fully furnished, mine for the night.

"Sure is nice to meet someone from California," he says.

I love it when a plan comes together.

The days through New York blend together. I camp on farmland most nights; sometimes I get lucky and find a patch of forest. Route 20 is straight but it's not flat, with some long grades made harder by the heat and the smothering backpack. Interesting characters along the way include Steve, who owns 80 acres and, in the winter, shoots at things outside his bedroom window while sipping coffee in bed. Wife doesn't seem to mind. I meet a girl in a black sundress who had a fight with friends and decided to walk the ten miles home, barefoot, in 90-degree weather. Get heckled by mean drunks in a bar. Pass the house of Glen, terminally ill and connected to an oxygen bottle, who tells me to "Live every day." A family cheers me on from their front yard while fist-pumping and screaming "America!" A construction worker buys me lunch and tells me I've got one more hill between here and the Rockies, and he's right.

In Cardiff I see a sign on the side of the road:

CARDIFF GIANT
DISINTERRED NEAR THIS VILLAGE ON
OCT. 16, 1869. REPRESENTED AS A
PETRIFIED PREHISTORIC MAN, IT WAS
SUBSEQUENTLY PROVED A HOAX.

The Cardiff Giant is one of the great hoaxes in American history, along with H.G Wells' *War of the Worlds* broadcast and anything that has to do with Scientology. Its story begins after George Hull, a cigar maker and an atheist, had a religious argument about the claim that there was once a race of giants inhabiting the earth, as stated in Genesis 6:4:

There were giants in the earth in those days; and also after that, when the sons of God came unto the daughters of men, and they bore children to them.

Hull decided to make his own giant, ordering a block of gypsum from Iowa, telling the carvers it was intended to be a monument to Abraham Lincoln. He apparently chose gypsum because the blue streaks running through it resembled human veins. He then hired a stonecutter to carve it into the likeness of a man, ten feet tall, making the artist and his assistants swear they wouldn't tell a soul. The statue was treated with sulfuric acid and buried in cow crap to make it look old. Finally, he had it shipped to Cardiff, where his cousin, William Newell, buried it on his farm. Workers were called in to "dig a well," and the giant fossil was unearthed by sheer, miraculous good fortune.

The petrified man was a sensation. Experts immediately dismissed it as a hoax while others thought it was an ancient statue, and some Christian fundamentalists hailed it as indisputable proof of the truth and accuracy of the Bible. William Newell put up a tent and charged 50 cents per person to view it. Crowds of people descended to do just that.

Hull eventually sold his interest in the statue — for a huge profit — and it was moved to Syracuse for display. Here it was seen by famous circus man and huckster extraordinaire P.T. Barnum, who tried to buy it. He was denied, so he had his own fossil made, displaying it in New York City while claiming his was the original and the other one a fake. This row gave rise to a famous saying attributed to Barnum but actually uttered by David Hannum, one of the owners of the "authentic" petrified man. "There's a sucker born every minute," Hannum said in regards to the throngs who lined up to pay Barnum for a viewing.

Hannum tried to sue Barnum in court, but the judge told him his fossil had to show up to testify about its own authenticity if the suit were to proceed.

Eventually Hull confessed to the hoax. The Cardiff Giant was bought by a man in Iowa to serve as a coffee table in his home. In 1947 it was sold to the Farmer's Museum in Cooperstown, where it now resides. Barnum's replica is on display in a museum in Detroit. To this day people still argue over which is the real fake and which is the fake fake.

Sometimes I get caught out. By "caught out" I mean misjudging the size of the town and getting stuck there at night trying to find a place to sleep. This happens in the town of Waterloo, New York, where I'm forced to knock on the door of a church just before sundown to ask if I can camp in the wet, tick-infested field a hundred yards behind the building. The pastor opens the door with an annoyed look on his face. Instead of saying, "Sure, as Jesus sheltered the poor and downtrodden, so shall I," he tells me to go to a campground ten miles the other way, with directions like this:

"Go two miles down the road, turn right at the big tree. Veer right at the rock that looks like a dinosaur then left at the old barn hidden in the trees, it's kind of hard to see. Go another five miles past the Moose Lodge . . ."

My mind begins to wander. I ponder the biblical consequences of kneeing a pastor in the nuts on the doorstep of his own church. But if this doesn't see me struck dead by lightning it will surely see me arrested by the local police, and as I've said, my prison days are behind me. I reconsider and walk into the night, muttering.

Generally, the more urban it gets, the less friendly people become. Typical is this interaction I have with a woman pruning her flowers in Seneca. For dramatic effect I've added what I assume she was thinking:

. . . What a beautiful day. But these darn aphids! They're ruining my azaleas. Hmm, there's a stranger on the sidewalk. Don't like strangers around here. Oh dear Lord — he has a backpack! A BACKPACK! Doris told me those people have fleas and steal vegetables from your garden. Can you imagine? I hope he doesn't stop to talk to me . . .

"Good morning. How are you?"

. . . Oh my goodness! He's stopping! And he's talking to me! Just look down and keep pruning. For God's sake keep pruning! . . .

"Beautiful flowers."

"Mmm."

"Have a nice day!"

"Yes."

. . . Thank God he's leaving! The nerve of him! Why don't the police do something? Doris told me . . .

So to recap, the two words she said were "mmm" and "yes," which mean nothing in the context of our non-conversation. It is possible that her cat died and she just doesn't feel like talking. But if that's the case, judging from the reactions of others I've met here, there are a lot of dead cats in this town.

South of Rochester I get my first injury as my leg mysteriously swells up below the knee, which makes walking difficult. So I spend the next three days recuperating in the city with old friends from the Griffen family, eating, sleeping, attending Fourth of July barbecues and behaving like a small child in the pool with other actual small children named Carsen and Emma. We play an underwater game I don't understand called "Invisible Dolphins."

"I'm an invisible dolphin."

"Okay."

"Now you're an invisible dolphin."

"Okay."

"Let's be invisible together."

"Okay."

I get the rest I'm looking for, except for the night I sleep beside "the doll room." Inhabiting said room are some of the creepiest dolls I've ever seen, in prairie dresses with uber-realistic features and moving eyeballs, nestled in a basket that looks distressingly like a tiny coffin. They're the kind of dolls you might find strolling around the house in the middle of the night, rummaging through your cutlery set as they go. My concern is the impending midnight bathroom run: stumble half asleep to the toilet, unzip, aim, hum softly to myself, tap, then turn around bleary-eyed to find two of them standing in the doorway with arms outstretched, whispering, "Come play with us . . . forever!" In the morning concerned friends will come looking, only to find an extra doll huddled corpse-like in its coffin — I mean basket — with the others. "Hey, that doll looks just like . . ."

It's hard leaving a bed and the company of good people for the uncertainty of the road. So it is this time. I say goodbye and by midday I feel so lonely it physically hurts, an empty spot in the middle of my chest. All I can do is walk. One foot in front of the other.

Head south from Lima. The days tick by. A pretty girl in the college town of Geneseo buys me pizza because she feels sorry for me. A not-so-pretty one tells me I smell, which is true but not very courteous. A deer screams at me in the forest at night. I get lost and walk in a circle for 12 miles. A fox runs into my campsite with a rabbit in its mouth.

At the Eagle Inn in Bliss, New York, my waitress is wearing flip-flops and a big smile. The historic final launch of the space shuttle Atlantis is on T.V. but someone wants to watch reruns of *The Price Is Right*, so they switch during lift-off. The non-speaking spokesmodel is wearing a tube top and stroking a jet ski, so I guess I'm in.

More strange people. Two guys, twenty-something, are getting screamed at by a third, much larger man. Something about a ruined lawnmower. The man yells for awhile then snaps, grabbing a tire iron and beating the crap out of the mower, one of those nice ones you sit in and drive around like a go-kart. He destroys the front end as I walk by, eyes straight ahead. Everyone goes quiet. I feel them watching me. As soon as I'm out of sight the screaming resumes, followed by the sound of more crunching metal.

Hypnotized by heat, hoping for rain but no lightning. These summer storms don't work that way. I crest a hill at sundown and see an incredible thing. A towering thunderhead, a black anvil, crushing the sky, destroying it, compressing it down upon the road in waves of shimmering heat, tendrils of rain swirling at its sides like tentacles, a living thing, lightning everywhere, no thunder. And at the very bottom a burning blue sun, aligned so perfectly with the road I can see my shadow for a quarter-mile down the double-yellow line. I stand there in the middle of the road with my arms in the air like a madman, like a moron, like a hero. And then it rains.

THE LAKE

The great lake is warm and brown, the beach littered with stones and slabs of shale. Electrical storms drift along a horizon as flat and infinite as that of the sea, barely perceptible where the dull metal of sky and water meet. A three-foot catfish lies dead on the beach, and as I float face-up on the surface I wonder what other monsters lurk in these muddy waters, hoping no one flushed a baby crocodile down the toilet 20 years ago. In the evening the wind comes up and the waves are waist high. I try bodysurfing but don't do so well, as I keep bumping off rocks on the bottom.

People say Lake Erie is so polluted it used to catch fire from all the oil floating on top. A man tells me *National Geographic* named this shore the third-best place in America for sunsets due to all the pollution drifting in from Gary, Indiana. Apparently, industrial pollutants bring out the reds and violets in the sky at the end of the day. Man improving upon nature once again. But I can't be concerned with flaming water and hungry crocodiles. I'm hot and I'm tired and I'm a dying man crawling through the desert. And I've found my water.

I follow the lakeshore as it curves into Pennsylvania. Plentiful campgrounds afford stress-free nights, but at a price. $23 to be exact. $18 at the state park, bumped up to $20 because I'm a non-resident, with a $3 check-in fee to maximize the fleecing. At another they only want $8, now we're talking, but it's essentially a junkyard inhabited by chain-smoking retirees in moldering caravans. Sanford and Son on vacation. Permanently. None of the toilet stalls close, so when nature calls it's a public spectacle. "Gather 'round everyone. Take a knee. Show's about to start."

The campground at Presque Isle State Park had me imagining silence, solitude and happy waves lapping at my toes. What it has is a water park on one side, a rollercoaster on the other and happy waves lapping at dozens of tents packed so tightly on the sand there's barely room to walk between them. Stupid me, I thought state parks were there to preserve nature. I ask the owner how much for a campsite, secretly hoping he'll quote me something outrageous so I have an excuse to grovel somewhere better, like the cemetery just down the road. He comes through, telling me with a straight face it's $32 a night, on the condition that I can find another spot on the beach large enough to set up a tent. Thankfully, I cannot.

The cemetery beckons. But before I have a chance to sneak in and make myself comfortable, I stumble upon the El Patio Motel. The pool party is just commencing.

"Is this place quiet?" I ask the manager.

"No."

Didn't even bother lying to me, which I appreciate. And it's the same price as the campground. Done.

Erie, Pennsylvania, comes in at number four on my "Do Not Return" list, narrowly edged out by Fargo, North Dakota; Gary, Indiana; and Flint, Michigan. Sadly, these Rust Belt towns I've walked through all look the same to me, like movie sets in which a neutron bomb has wiped out the population but left the buildings standing, if barely. A ring of suburbs gives way to car dealerships and fast food joints encircling an empty, rotten core of abandoned factories and vacant lots, Frankenstein cities with the heart cut out but limbs still twitching and lurching along. Boarded-up homes like rows of skulls with broken windows for eyes and mouths of kicked-in doors. Front yards sprout discarded liquor bottles but no grass. Waterlogged sofas sit on the sidewalks. Lots of people standing around in the middle of the day arguing or doing nothing, and lots of guys with their pants pulled down. On purpose. People warn me to be off the street by sundown, which would have seemed laughable for a city this small. Until I walked through it.

My last day on the lake, and in Pennsylvania, is spent watching my toes bob in the brown muck, thinking about that flushed crocodile again. Despite its shortcomings I love this huge lake, this inland sea. There's something about water so big you can't see across it, so big it tricks you into believing it's the ocean. I love that I'll never know half of what's down inside it. I love that it still has mysteries. As the sun dips into the far edge, that much-hyped pollution from Indiana does its thing, and the sky lights up in hyper-saturated hues of orange, red and magenta. There's a cheer from the bluff above. But it's not for the chemically enhanced sunset. It's for two shirtless, middle-aged blobs with cigars in their mouths who are driving golf balls into the water from the top of their RV. People with bellies and pink shoulders stand around the bottom with red plastic cups in hand, swaying and jiggling. A bad, early 80s power ballad blares from a stereo. The sun sinks into the lake.

OHIO

Take away the cooling breezes of the lake and the heat becomes unbearable. The temperature shoots up into the high 90s, then well over 100 for days on end. The heat index, or what the temperature feels like when the wind stops and the humidity kicks in, is as high as 108, even 111 degrees on the hottest days.

The air smells like grass and cow turds, with heavy moisture that settles on my neck like a blanket. The same angry sun that sank red into a cornfield last night now rises silver and new on the other side of the road, burning away the mist, gearing up for another round of torture. By 11 a.m. I can barely move. Now, instead of daydreaming about beautiful women slathering me with ice cream cones on tropical beaches, I fantasize about endless convoys of trucks and motor homes roaring past, knowing each one will provide four to five seconds of cooling breeze as they rush by. But right now the only things on the road are Ford Fiestas and tiny European imports, and the only way they'll provide relief is if I lie down in the middle of the highway and have them run me over.

My pack feels like an overcoat. The heat forces me to carry extra water, which just adds more weight. I sit in the shade of trees or grain silos waiting for a cloud to pass overhead, then follow in its shadow until it fades or outraces me and I'm forced to hide, vampire-like, from the naked, merciless, unblinking eye of the sun. I pray for rain.

But be careful what you wish for, because when it rains, it comes in buckets and explosions of electricity, born of towering anvils like the one I walked through days ago. The mornings start out the same, hazy yet clear, but if any hint of cloud appears by midday I know what's coming. Humidity rises, and the fluffy white cotton balls drifting innocently overhead coalesce into sinister black curtains from which angry gods spit thunder and hurl bolts of white lightning. I rush into the forest and pitch my tent in the thickest stand of trees I can find, figuring the odds of being hit decrease that way. Then I sit, again in my underwear because it's still too hot, trying to gauge if the thunder is getting farther away or closer, counting the moments from flash to rumble. Five seconds . . . three . . . two.

The storm is in the forest now, lightning arcs across the sky several times a second. I could read by its light. The ground shudders. Leaves, pine needles and insects avalanche down upon the tent from wind-lashed treetops. The sky opens, rain pours in. The water line outside the tent rises two inches. I feel like I'm sitting on a waterbed. Rain lasts for twenty minutes. Then it stops, wind dies to nothing, and the last rays of the sun pierce the forest in horizontal shafts of light, reflecting off leaves and branches, filling the shadows with a diffused golden glow. An ancient light, the kind you'd see streaming through the yellowed glass of a centuries-old cathedral.

Steam rises from moss and leaf litter on the ground. Raindrops tap the roof of my tent. Insects and worms begin to stir on the forest floor. Then the light fades, the forest grows dark and menacing. The tapping on my roof increases, gently at first, then violently. Thunder and lightning return, the gods angrier than before. I ride through waves of storm and wind as the night progresses. My little tent leaks but holds, a ravaged ark tossed but not broken.

Weaving around these storms, I stumble into Canton and find a bad motel. Bad as in cheap. The Towne Manor. The sign is straight out of 1950s Las Vegas. Inside, the manager sits at a counter behind very thick glass. A regulations sheet is posted there. Rule Number Four states:

ABSOLUTELY NO BEGGING, PANHANDLING OR
BOTHERING OTHER MOTEL GUESTS

The room smells like mold and cigarettes. All I want is a mattress and the remote. Remote? Who am I kidding? The T.V. is older than I am. The backpack will be sealed in a trash bag and put up on the table to keep the insects out, because frankly I'm more concerned about bed bugs here than I am about ticks in the forest. Are those prostitutes across the street?

McDonald's, how I love thee. Actually, under normal circumstances I avoid thee like the plague, equating the health risk from your gut-enhancing, artery-clogging fare to be on par with that of cigarette smoking. But that's under normal circumstances. These are desperate times. Many a blazing afternoon I've trudged down that empty road, dehydrated and probably minutes away from heat stroke, resigned to nibbling the crusts of three-day-old bread slices (because the middles have molded away) and sucking on a lemon drop for moisture, only to crest that last hill to find you sitting on the corner of some minor intersection, you and that lonely gas station opposite, gleaming in the sun like a fairy princess and her ugly

53

sister, welcoming me to your bosom as a mother would a son come home from war. Your near-total fast food domination has made you my go-to place for all-purpose loitering, a golden-arched sanctuary of WiFi, air conditioning and endless fountain drinks. Thank you, mother. I love you.

Thus I find myself in your embrace, yet again, outside Canton. I cut off a pack of school children making for the last available booth and settle in for long hours of lounging. A group of old men is making noise in the next booth, talking and gesturing about some teenage girls across the restaurant. It's locker room talk — 7th grade locker room talk. The combined age of these geriatric perverts would stretch back to the time of Columbus, yet they're talking about girls young enough to be their granddaughters, great-granddaughters even.

I've come to believe that many people have an emotional default position, a spot reached in their personal evolution in which they go no further, despite all that talk about limitless human potential and constantly expanding one's horizons. I'm that way myself. I still like to burn things. Flatulence will always be funny. I occasionally say "dude," but I'm working on it.

These guys peaked at about 14. As they're describing, loudly and in detail, what they would do with these teenage girls if they still had a shot, a man pulls up in the drive-thru and stares absently into the restaurant, lost in thought. One of the coffin-stuffers flips him off because, as he says to no one in particular, "I don't like assholes staring at me." The man in the drive thru throws his hands in the air and rolls forward.

No, wisdom doesn't always come with age. Some people are poised, gracious and wise at 16, while others go through entire lives learning nothing, dropping out at a fast food restaurant and giving the finger to customers in the drive-thru with other toothless old monkeys. An evolutionary dead end, the last of the Neanderthals. I close my eyes to make them go away. When I open them they're still sitting there, and one is looking right at me. I turn back to my hamburger before he can flip me off.

Today I meet the Amish.

For weeks I've been stomping through horse crap and seeing telltale scuff marks from buggy wheels on the side of the road, but the people who left them have been like ghosts. Now Lenny, the chief of police in the town of Wilmot, tells me I'm about to enter the Amish capital of the world.

The Amish fascinate me, as I assume they would fascinate anyone who has had no experience with them. How do you exist in modern America and choose to live, in varying degrees, in the 18th century? If I was braver and a lot dumber, I'd ask, "So what's it like to be Amish?" To which they would reply, "I really just want to watch T.V. and play on the computer. And that's a stupid question."

There are a quarter-million Amish in America, and they are one of the fastest growing populations in the world due to their belief in large families, which they view as a gift from God. Arrived from Europe in the early 1700s, first in Pennsylvania, then fanning out west. There are dozens of different sects. The most conservative of the Old Order Amish use no electricity and no indoor plumbing. They finish school after the eighth grade. Many dress in black, men wearing beards after marriage but no moustaches, which they associate with the military and therefore forbid. Some households forbid musical instruments, and some won't even use the red reflective triangles on the backs of their buggies because they consider them to be too worldly. They speak Pennsylvania Dutch, actually a dialect of German. They call the non-Amish "English." But the most liberal groups, like the Beachy Amish, drive cars and use electricity.

The non-Amish I speak to — the "English" like me — either shrug or rant when I ask about the Amish, but I suppose you find that everywhere when vastly different groups live so close to one another. Some people tell me to look for drunk and doped-up Amish teenagers having sex in cornfields and warn me to watch out on the road because I'm likely to get run over by a drunk Amish kid behind the wheel of a car for the first time. A man at a convenience store tells me the teenagers are constantly in heat. Aren't all teenagers?

"They'll hump your leg if you let 'em," he warns, and he's not joking.

I think what they're talking about is *rumspringa*, or "running around." This is the period in which Amish adolescents are allowed to experience the world around them, and all the temptations and vices inherent in it, before being baptized and formally returning to the church as adults. Many of them have pre-marital sex and experiment with smoking, alcohol, and even illegal drugs. But I'm doubtful it's the non-stop Roman orgy many people make it out to be.

I have made an important purchase, one that will unwittingly nudge the door open when dealing with the Amish. It's a straw hat for $5.99 at a convenience store. At best it makes me look like a soccer dad, at worst like a lampshade. But it's a huge improvement over the stupidly black hat I had before, whose only advantage was making me look roguish and slightly dangerous, which all men secretly want to be. Otherwise it just turned my brain into a baked potato whenever the sun came out.

An added advantage of my new hat is that from a distance it makes me look vaguely Amish, or so I'm told by Marlon, who wanders out from his metal-working shop with his five young children to investigate.

"It *is* your hat, man," he says with a German accent. "You look like one of us."

I ask him if we can trade hats for a minute and he looks around sheepishly, as if he's not really supposed to, but then relents.

"Perfect," he says after we hand-off and have a look at one another.

His young daughter, who has been clinging to her father's leg, blue dress and blonde hair blowing in the breeze, points at my kneecaps and starts laughing.

Marlon eyes me from head to toe and frowns. "She is right, these pants will not do," he says, pointing at my shorts and exposed legs.

"Well, I'm only half-Amish," I explain, which he finds extremely funny, or maybe he's just humoring me. On the spot I decide to make that line my standard dumb joke when dealing with Amish men. Turns out Marlon is the exception, because most others just stare at me and nod when I say it, as if I were discussing the price of hay. Or they really believe I'm a wayward brother on walkabout. Some just look confused. But conversation usually follows.

Like Lenny said, Winesburg and Berlin are at the center of the Amish universe. This is their country, or a somewhat touristy version of it. Buses from Cleveland and Columbus disgorge tourists by the dozens to stay at high end "traditional" hotels and dine in overpriced restaurants. But all it takes is a short journey off the main highway to find the real deal. I buy dinner cakes from women in blue dresses and bonnets on the side of the road. Stores have hitching posts for horses and roads are extra wide to accommodate buggies on the shoulders. Signs outside farmhouses advertise fresh eggs or handmade furniture for sale but always end with "Please do not disturb on Sunday." There are no power lines. Buggies sit on dirt or gravel driveways where cars should be. The name "Yoder" is ubiquitous on store fronts and signs. I eavesdrop on street corner conversations and it sounds like a form of pidgin, with English and German words mixing together.

DAY 44

Fog rolls in before dawn. Street lights hover in the mist like alien saucers. Barren trees from a dead and drowned forest lean precariously in swamps like tombstones broken by a flood. A large grey heron is hunting frogs, and geese leave trails as they swim across the water, which is bright green with some sort of floating plant, like tiny lily pads covering the surface of the water by the millions.

A woodchuck runs into the road. It stops and stares at the sky, pensively, as if contemplating the vastness of it and the shapes of clouds drifting past. Really just looking for hawks, I suppose. A car bears down upon it from the rear. The driver swerves, and the woodchuck goes perfectly between the tires — frozen, seemingly unconcerned — emerging unscathed on the other side still looking at the sky. Another car comes and the same thing happens, woodchuck still standing in the middle of the lane. But behind it is a semi. The truck swerves like the others, woodchuck goes through the front tires. All he has to do is stand there watching the clouds and he'll make it, but no, the truck is too long, and after a second he bolts for the forest and goes under the double tires of the trailer with a horrible sound I've never heard before, a sound I won't describe. The truck — cold, metallic, indifferent — grinds away up the hill. I walk out and stand over the little woodchuck, watching him die. There's no discernible damage. He looks calm. Peaceful. Like he's napping. Then he gasps for air, inhaling three more times, before his chest relaxes and eyes glass over, and he's gone. I stand there a long time. A moment ago he was running through the grass, beautiful, perfect, and now he's road kill. Where did he go to? What happened to him, to that spark, that soul, that thing that animates him, animates us, makes us breathe, makes us alive? Where does it go to so suddenly?

A half hour later I come across a tiny, iridescent green hummingbird sitting on the road, propped up, wings out, holding his beak up like he's trying to breathe, head bobbing up and down. A windshield casualty. I'm sure he's finished and consider putting him out of his misery. But as I lift my foot over him he turns his head to look at it, waiting, the last thing he'll ever see, and I can't do it. I gather him up in my fingers, very gently, and place him in the shade on the side of the road, hoping he'll pull together a miracle and fly away. But as I walk off I know I've just replaced a quick death with a slow one when the ants and the sun find him. But all I do is walk away faster.

I spend the rest of the day with my head down, watching my feet plod across the tar and gravel on the side of the road. Think pointless thoughts about life and death and the beginning of time and the borders of the universe, about exploding stars and dying hummingbirds, the far shore of the earth and what lies beyond. Things too big for me. The sorts of things explained by religion in a thousand different comforting or terrifying ways, never coming to a consensus. I think about my father, who was hospitalized with a staph infection that got into his bloodstream just before I was set to leave on my first attempt at this walk. About getting to the hospital as the doctor says, "You better see him now," because he is that close to dying. In the ICU, isolated in his own room, a room that smells like Latex and piss, beneath a Christmas tree of tubes, IV bags and blinking green LCDs. Television on with no sound and no one watching. Holding his swollen hand, marveling at how such a fragile body could contain the strength of the spirit I knew lived within. I asked the same questions then. Where are you? Are you still there? Or are you somewhere I can't go? Stay a little longer. Stay long enough to see me succeed, to make you proud. Stay so the woman you have loved for half a century will not live out her life alone and frightened. Come back a while longer. Come back.

And he did. After ten days lying unconscious in that miserable, sterile place, the last place you'd want to see before you leave this world, he came back.

I look up from my shoes. Hawks are circling on updrafts. The road winds through the forest, climbs a hill, emerges into brilliant sun shining on cornfields. It dips beside the river and disappears around a corner.

THE MIDWEST

On the outskirts of Columbus the rudeness begins, the fear, the suspicion, like it always does when I get near cities. Stuck at a stop sign because I don't know which street to take. Cars roll by, drivers either ignoring me or waving me off dismissively, running the stop sign so they won't have to talk to me, pretending they're on cell phones. After five or six cars a black BMW edges up. I wave hopefully. Through a crack in the window a blond woman barks, "What do you want?" So I tell her, and, obviously irritated, she yells something while accelerating through the intersection to emphasize her disdain. I lay a curse upon her, many years of continued financial success sitting in a large office behind a large desk, driving an ever more expensive car to and from that same stressful job for decades to come while the noose tightens, the wrinkles form and the walls close in. I walk by a house and see another woman, this one not blonde but enormous, standing in her doorway with hands on hips, staring at me. I wave. Nothing. Say hello. Nothing. Wave again . . . Her head turns slowly to follow me as I walk by. Finally I stop, turn toward her and put my hands on my hips to mimic her. We stand there for several seconds, a pair of idiots facing off. Then she shakes her head, waves her hand in disgust and slams the door. My feelings exactly.

All through Ohio I've been weaving around cities, trying my best to stay out of them. Now I'm in Columbus, the most populous city in the state. Ahead are five days off with friends, my biggest break of the journey. I am taken in by Barbara and Don, the parents of my maybe girlfriend. They say make yourself at home. So I do. I eat a lot. Perfect the art of lounging. Nap in the afternoon. Make a big decision.

That decision is to get a baby jogger. I knew this day was coming. Only I didn't think it would come so soon. I thought I'd make it to western Kansas at least. But this heat has forced me to carry a lot of extra water much sooner than I expected. That weight and the smothering pack have forced the issue. I need another solution. And even after nearly dying with my cart last year, and swearing I'd never do it again, I knew in the back of my mind I'd have to get the weight off my back and onto something else to get across those vast, dry, lonely deserts. A cart, or something else with wheels.

The main problem, as before, is that the jogger will put me another 1 1/2 feet onto the road. Not so easy to jump to the side when approaching drivers are sleeping, texting, or just angry and impatient with the bum getting in the way. But I'm good at rationalizing. My path is essentially flat and straight for a thousand miles. By staying on U.S. routes with big shoulders, or empty country roads, it should be safe enough. As safe as riding a bicycle across the country, and people do that all the time. I don't have much choice anyway.

But what to get? I don't have the time or ability to customize another cart on the road. It will have to be a something already made and easy to assemble — a baby jogger.

Notice I said "baby jogger." Not stroller. I make the distinction to protect my own fragile ego, which just won't stand for looking like a total nut job by pushing a *baby stroller* down the highway. A jogger is perfectly acceptable. You run with it; you don't stroll.

I go to Buybuy Baby with Barbara, my surrogate mom. The store is a clearinghouse of all things baby. At the front are about a dozen different models of joggers, lined up like fancy European sports cars. Some are for twins (too big). Some have low weight capacities (need at least 70 pounds). Some have wimpy plastic wheels (no good for off-roading). Then I see it. The Summit XC. Sleek. Sexy. 80-pound weight capacity. Front wheel that locks or can be swiveled for maneuverability and handling. Lots of trunk space. Handbrake. Tough but stylish. And it says Baby *Jogger* right on the front. It's love.

Barbara insists on paying for part of it. I love my surrogate mom. I fold it in half, another beautiful feature, and shove it in the car. The only thing missing is the "Real Men Drive Baby Joggers" bumper sticker. My rugged good looks will have to do.

I'm not yet done loafing but have to leave the Robinsons early because they're off to see a real baby, their grandson Ben, who's less than a year old and adorable but makes my list anyway for getting me kicked out of the house. So I find a new nest with friends of friends — Colin, Heather and their daughter, Juno, who live a short seven-mile stumble south near the center of the city.

Colin is a bit of a Renaissance man, father and Ph.D. student by day, drummer in a punk band by night. The whole family seems hyper-intelligent, to the point that I just nod and say "uh-huh" a lot during conversations because I'm not quite sure what they're talking about. Juno is the same way; I imagine her up in her room reading Shakespeare or doing calculus for fun at an age when I was still blowing up GI Joes with firecrackers and frying ants in the sand box with a magnifying glass.

I stay for three days. Longer than that makes it too hard to leave. A roof, a couch and a refrigerator — my weaknesses. I pry myself off the inflatable mattress and say goodbye.

Homeless, or not homeless? That is the question as me and my little burro roll down High Street into the city center. Several guys with twigs in their hair and bits of toilet paper in their beards ask for change, which I guess indicates they don't think I'm one of them. But then another asks for drugs (or a "switch," as he calls it) which I'm pretty sure means he does indeed think I'm on the streets.

I've never seen so many tattoo parlors. I'm told they survive, despite the competition, thanks to thousands of incoming Ohio State freshman, who, finally freed from the clutches of mommy and daddy, go on to celebrate their new freedom by blowing mommy's and daddy's money on something they'll regret in a few years.

Make a right on West Broad Street, look down the boulevard between high rises to open fields in the distance, a canyon of glass and steel opening up to a broad plain. Outside the city this street becomes U.S. Route 40, a straight shot west for hundreds of miles. I knock off the first 28 and finish at one of my go-to camping options — a cemetery. The jogger has paid off already, as I end the day for the first time with my feet not swollen or in substantial pain. My neck feels great, and without the pack on my back I can walk in the heat and humidity without much problem. The potential for consistent 30-mile days is now there.

I park at the edge of the graveyard behind some mounds of dirt — what could those be for? — so as to not seem too disrespectful if someone were to find me here or the dead were to suddenly rise for a midnight stroll and find me blocking the exits. I sit on a bench in the central gazebo, writing and watching thunderstorms float by.

My neighbors in the cemetery behave as I'd hoped they would — quiet and not inclined to visit — and the night passes without incident. In the morning I roll out and in a few hours come to a spot where the jogger reveals its major limitation. Past the town of Phoneton the road goes over a dam and the shoulder vanishes. There's a 60-foot drop-off to the side, and a guardrail forcing me further into traffic. Even without the jogger this would be dangerous, but with it I am right in the road. There's a lot of traffic and people are getting angry, to the point that they don't want to slow down at all to safely pass. They roll up to within ten feet, then gun the engine as they pass just to show me how mad they are. Which of course makes it more dangerous. It gets so bad I take my pack out of the jogger, throw it on my back, then fold the jogger in half and carry it over my head to reduce my profile. The dam is two miles long and the jogger weighs 25 pounds. This is not easy. And it's still too dangerous.

Thirty minutes later I make it to the other side. And there, waiting for me, are not one, not two, but four police cars from three separate law enforcement agencies — city police, highway patrol and state troopers. Standing beside each vehicle is at least one officer with his hands on his hips, in the same way my mother used to do when I'd done something stupid and she was unhappy with me.

'Sir, are you in need of assistance?" says the closest one.
"No, I'm okay."

"Glad to hear that." Pause. "Sir, could you please tell me precisely what it is that you're doing?"

"Um . . . I'm walking across America."

He sighs, then looks over his shoulder at the other officers, as if to say, "I told you he was an idiot." Then they start laughing.

"We thought it was something like that," he says. "We got a call from a concerned citizen saying a vagrant was collecting cans in the middle of the road."

"A vagrant?" I ask.

"That would be you, sir," he says. "I think 'crazy vagrant' were the exact words."

This will be the first of many times I hear something like this. In the coming weeks it will become clear that there are some basic labels people apply to me. When rolling through towns, I am "Crazy Homeless Man Looking for Things to Steal." On the highway, I become "Crazy Homeless Man Collecting Cans in the Middle of the Road," (why am I always "in the middle of the road?"). When I stop to take a leak, leaving the jogger visible but unattended on the shoulder of the road, I transform into "Crazy Homeless Man Passed Out Drunk and/or Dead in the Bushes." But the most common persona, the one I knew I'd assume as soon as I took a baby jogger out on the road in 98-degree heat with big rigs blowing by at 80 miles an hour, is "Crazy Homeless Father Trying to Kill Baby."

The police officer, still laughing, asks for my ID.

"California!" he says when he sees it, with a "that-explains-it" tone in his voice. He runs it and it comes up clean.

"You have a good day, sir. And by the way, there's another dam a few miles down the road . . ."

That's just swell. There is another dam, with the road on top as long and narrow as the first, a straight, raised berm with a long line of cars going in either direction. I'm not walking on this thing, and I'm not carrying a 25-pound jogger above my head either. Luckily, unlike the first dam, this one has a detour. There's no water behind it, just a wooded tangle called Englewood Park, which presumably becomes Englewood Lake whenever it rains too much. I bomb down the side with the jogger and find a trail winding through the trees. The park is a wild beauty, with the best forest camping I've seen in weeks. Of course there's a sign: NO CAMPING ALLOWED. A travesty. To rectify the situation, I stash my gear behind a tree, head into town for a spaghetti dinner, then sneak back in after dark to camp.

Next day a very old man is sipping coffee outside a convenience store on the edge of town. Seems a bit crazy, muttering to himself but aware enough to smile and say hello. He announces, for no apparent reason, that he has been working for 73 years and is damn well entitled to sit around drinking coffee and doing nothing. I agree. Then he stands up and starts doing half-hearted karate kicks and shadow-boxing to show he still has it, which he clearly doesn't, because he can barely move and I swear I hear celery stalks crunching whenever he does. Very entertaining, but I have to repeat everything I say three times and he keeps asking me where my baby is, so I say goodbye and move on.

By the end of the day I'm half a mile from Indiana. I can see it from here. Looks just like Ohio. Up the road at a truck stop I sit down for dinner, eavesdropping on a few conversations to find out what real truckers talk about. Seems to be seven things: women, coffee, women, football, women, stupid drivers and women. I order a salad and the waitress brings me something that looks like it was a head of lettuce in a former life before someone threw it under a lawnmower, collected the shavings and placed a sliver of radish the size of a toenail clipping on top.

Back at the campground I sit for awhile with Leon and his three dogs — Charley, Cowboy and Mario — who are painted together bigger than life-size on the side of his RV beneath the words, "Somewhere Over the Rainbow: Leon's Boys." As I'm thinking of jumping into the stagnant, murky, half-drained swimming hole, because once again it's so hot it's hard to breathe, Leon throws some crumbs into it and on cue three giant catfish rise to the surface to gulp them down while Charley, Cowboy and Mario bark themselves hoarse on the bank. Those things live in the swimming hole? To someone like me, who thinks any fish over three feet is a shark, this is very bad. Dark or murky water is also off limits, even if it's in a swimming pool. No telling what's hiding down there. It's a deal-breaker. I'll sweat on the ground with the dogs. Just before sundown the camp owner, who goes by the quintessential American name of Bob Smith, tells me I'll be mugged at soon as I cross the state line into Richmond. I guess Indiana is a whole lot rougher than Ohio.

INDIANA

Observations from a $29.95 motel room:

-There is no such thing as "non-smoking."

-The carpet is so thoroughly stained it looks like an Impressionist painting, possibly a Monet. Or, more accurately, if Monet were to paint a pizza, this is what it would look like.

-The deadbolt has been moved/replaced no less than four times, apparently because that's how many times the door has been kicked in.

-Their business plan should end with the words "insurance fire."

-The parking lot is woefully inadequate at accommodating the seven police cars currently trying to pull in.

You read that correctly — seven police cars. And this time they're not even here for me. I'm torn between barricading myself in the bathroom or risking a bullet to the head by cracking the door to see what's going on. Feeling brave, I opt for a trip to the Coke machine so I can rubberneck from a safe distance. There's drama outside Room 119, three tiny rooms down from mine. A very large, disheveled man in boxer shorts with no shirt and no shoes is being lectured by a police officer about "being a man" and "breaking his habit," while two women cry in the doorway and fellow officers stand around with their hands on their holsters. I want to ask my delightful neighbors if they know what's going on, but I don't want to end up starring in an episode of "Cops" as the guy lying on the ground under a yellow tarp, so I just go back to my room and start piling furniture in front of the door. Only eight hours until sun up.

It's probably unfair to say I hate Indianapolis, but I hate Indianapolis. I'm looking for an oasis, a respite from corn and wheat and fences. I won't find it here. Indianapolis, at least this part of it, is the usual strip mall hell followed by another version of the decay I saw in Erie, Warren and Canton. Only there's a lot more of it. Thirty miles more. Did Peyton Manning really live here all those years?

I'm at a low point. The jogger, my little burro, my friend, my confidant, has made things easier, but I'm still struggling with the fences and "No Trespassing" signs that keep me from sleeping anywhere in peace. Each night I expect to be rousted by police or angry farmers, or to wake up tied to a table, with cleavers and meat hooks dangling above me, waiting to have my organs harvested in a basement by some guy in suspenders and a bloody apron. People have been yelling at me out their car windows, usually "Jackass!" or something like that. It's been happening for the past week or so, maybe just people thinking I'm trying to kill my nonexistent baby again. I wave to everyone, and for the first time not many wave back.

Things come to a head in Indianapolis. I leave the aforementioned crack motel and stumble just ten more miles to another one, because I just don't feel like walking today. The Relax Inn, it's called, though you'd never know it from the sign, which sits on a pole out front hanging in tatters like a shredded billboard. I take a picture of it and title it "After the Apocalypse, Study #1," because that's exactly what it looks like. A man pounds on my door yelling about a cigarette, so I tell him to piss off and he comes back two hours later yelling the same thing. A couple next door screams and fights all day, and I think the pogo-stick club is meeting in the room above me. I sit in front of the T.V. with the drapes closed.

If I had a cause, as many people told me I should, this walk would be easier. When things got really tough I'd just let go of my own reasons and let my cause push me forward. "Do it for the kids!" I'd say, when I could no longer do it for myself. But I don't have a charity. Maybe I could have found one, but I'd be in it for the wrong reasons. I might raise a little money, but I'd really just be cashing in on the publicity that would make this journey easier — someone reading about me in the local newspaper and setting me up with a couch or a comped motel room to assist me in my noble endeavor. I'd be spiritually dishonest, the worst kind of deceit.

I have no higher purpose. There is no cause. The cause is me.

I remind myself that life is beautiful. I turn off the T.V. and walk out the door.

Another night, another overpriced campground. The worst so far. I'm still in the suburbs of Indianapolis and don't feel like groveling behind a dumpster, so here I am. The camp office is decorated with bucolic scenes of people reeling in fish from streams and gazing admiringly at forested vistas. Other photos show happy old people playing bingo and children running around in a pumpkin patch. Bingo? Pumpkin patch? This looks bad.

The smiling, grandmotherly woman at the desk stops smiling and looks a lot less grandmotherly as soon as I walk in. She doesn't ask what I'm doing, because she doesn't want to know. I tell her anyway in the hope that she'll take pity on me and not rob me blind. I am incorrect.

"That'll be $35."

Thirty-five dollars. To lie down in the dirt for the night like a dog. I've been taken advantage of like this a few times already. I'm not happy. Not-so-kind grammy senses my rising indignation and hastily starts listing the many useless amenities I'd be getting for my money.

"There's fishing in the stream, and since you're staying with us you don't have to pay for that (it's usually $7). Out back on the deck we're having music! It's rock and roll night tonight! Everyone sings along! Tickets are $5. There are hayrides for the children, and fireworks at 9:30! The shower block is right next to the tent area. It's only $2 for a shower . . ."

I drop my head on the counter in total exasperation. It makes a noticeable thud.

Not-so-kind grandpa, who has been whittling or God-knows-what in the corner, steps up to the counter.

"There's a problem here, bucko?"

I look at him and sigh. Grammy's standing next to him with her arms folded across her chest and a "tsk-tsk" look on her face. A couple other "campers" — I use the term loosely — are standing around like cattle, waiting to see what will happen next. I take a few steps to the door. But wait a minute — did he really just call me "bucko?"

I turn around.

"Yeah, there's a problem. I asked to set up a tent. That's all. I just want to lie down on the ground and sleep. There's no way it costs 35 bucks to do that. Do you think Jesus would charge me 35 bucks to sleep on the ground?" I say, gesturing at the half-dozen crucifixes on the wall.

Grammy and Pappy are turning red. The two cattle swaying in line beside me are utterly speechless, staring at me with mouths agape. Pappy tries to speak, but he's so angry he just stammers.

"Now . . . you . . . listen — "

I do not listen.

" . . . And I don't want a hayride. Do I look like I want a hayride? Do you see any kids with me? Do I look like I'm carrying a fishing pole? And why the hell would I want to pay five extra bucks to listen to your crappy music? And you're going to charge me two bucks for a shower after stealing thirty-five? Yes, there is a problem."

Pappy is spitting all over himself. Grammy has her hand on her forehead, like she's going to faint, looking distressed instead of ashamed, which is what they both should be for attempted robbery like this. Pappy continues frothing, something about the police, but I cut him off again.

" . . . And don't ever call me 'bucko.'"

I push past the gaping cattle, doing my best to ignore the "Please do not slam door!" sign on my way out. My little jogger is waiting for me on the deck, rainwater dripping miserably off her handlebars and mud-splattered belly. Now I've done it. I lost my temper and I made a scene. Grammy's probably had a fainting spell and Pappy's reaching for the shotgun under the counter. And I've assured myself of a miserable night under a bridge or a bus stop. But you know what? That felt *good*. I'd like to think I've evolved past the point of senseless confrontation . . . but who am I kidding? That felt really good.

I wipe the rain from my eyes and put my hat on. My little jogger brightens noticeably when she sees me. I hum softly to myself as I take her by the reins and lead her down the muddy drive, past the concert deck where the crappy sing-along will take place, past the playground, the miniature golf course and out the gate. Sometime after sunset we find a small culvert under the road, a miserable muddy spot full of cobwebs and graffiti. We will suffer here. This is what you get for standing on principle. Yet I've had a small revelation: I have what I need. All that I need. At this worst of times, standing in the mud and broken glass, green algal scum seeping from the walls overhead, watching black sheets of rain drown out the evening, I don't feel lost. I don't feel alone, like I'm adrift at sea with so far to go and no guarantee of getting there. The path will always be uncertain, until the day I die. But I have what I need — a pair of legs, an iron will and a spirit that will not break. A pagan, naked and bruised, godless and free. And home is where I lay my head down.

Indiana is what I thought it would be — cornfields on top of cornfields. I sleep in them nearly every night, asking permission when possible, ducking in when not. Sometimes I sleep beneath radio antennas or power substations, any place that limits my sense of trespassing but affords a flat, hidden spot. The nights are humid and hot, but after sundown a breeze picks up that rustles the stalks of corn and sends me off to sleep.

I cross the state in a week, doing 30-35 miles a day. In this part of Indiana there are still forests, with a few drowned quarries and hidden lakes. I pass a prison and see guards in the towers watching me through binoculars, probably wondering if I'm going to make a suicide run and blow a hole in the wall with my explosive-laden baby jogger. I wave at them and they wave back. A silly dog follows me, darting into cornfields, crouching down with his butt in the air like he's stalking me, then pouncing when I walk by. He does this with cars as well. I don't think he's going to live long.

I think if I hear one more person say, not nicely, in an accusatory tone while pointing at the jogger, "There better not be a baby in there!" I'm going to punch him in the face. So to keep myself out of jail, or from getting punched in the face right back, I've decided to make a sign to clarify things. I buy a piece of white vinyl and an indelible black marker at a sign shop in Terre Haute. What should my sign say? It seems pretty obvious that anyone with half a brain and a hint of observational skills could tell I'm not carrying a baby. So I'm inclined to make a sign playing off their hysteria and lack of good sense. Options include "I USED TO HAVE A BABY BUT IT CRAWLED AWAY" and "NO BABY HERE BUT I'LL GLADLY TAKE YOURS." Or I could just draw a picture of a baby with a big red "X" through it. But then people would think I hate babies, which is entirely untrue as long as they're not crying. Or I could just say what I'm thinking — "WHAT THE HELL ARE YOU GAWKING AT?"

I wait a few hours until my head clears, then settle on something a little less confrontational:

"WALK AMERICA. AND NO, I HAVE NO BABY."

DAY 67

Walking through Brownstown I hear tires screech up ahead. A beaten old car, something from the 80s, might be a Celica, with duct tape where the windows should be, is peeling out in reverse straight at me. It pulls up alongside and two guys jump out, both in dirty wife-beaters and jeans, shaved heads, looking kind of scary. One guy has a scar running over the top of his skull from ear to ear. He's definitely had his head cut open but I don't ask. He comes out screaming and gesturing wildly.

"Are you shittin' me?!"

No, I'm not, I'm really walking across America.

"You're shittin' me!"

It's the sign. The sign is working. I've had more people honk, wave, and pull over to talk in the past three days than in the previous two weeks. Some people are still afraid of me, still hysterical, which is fine. They might see me as stupid and irresponsible — guilty as charged — while in return I can write them off as narrow-minded and lacking any sense of adventure. Through generalization and stereotyping we come to understand each other. Regardless, the people who are interested are taking the time to let me know.

Just then the guy's phone rings and he screams into it.

"Remember that dumbass we saw walking on 40 with the baby stroller? Yeah . . . yeah . . . well guess what? He ain't no dumbass!"

It's the sign.

ILLINOIS

Some people live quiet lives. They mind their own business. See the doctor regularly, drive a car with nice airbags. Fortify their home with burglar alarms, bars on the windows and guard dogs out front. Safe. Secure. Then an airplane falls out of the sky and lands in their living room.

I cheat death every day. A white line painted on the asphalt separates me from tons of metal and glass flying by at 80 miles an hour, wind-blown semis and catatonic RV drivers missing me by two feet. I'm a toddler playing on a freeway. A crash test dummy. A matador teasing 60,000-pound bulls. And I just keep walking away.

The National Road is testing my mortality. Through Ohio, Indiana and Illinois, U.S. Route 40 is called the National Road because it is built atop a much older road of the same name, the first federally funded long-distance road in America, begun in 1811 at Cumberland, Maryland. During the 1920s it became one of the original coast-to-coast U.S. Highways. Through the last two states the National Road has been a perfect walking road, with wide shoulders and few trucks. In Illinois those shoulders disappear. The highway has essentially been replaced by Interstate 70, which it parallels as it crosses the state. Now it's treated more like a county road than a trans-continental one, which means shoulders and upkeep are no longer a priority. The road becomes dangerous, and I consider taking long detours to find a safer route. In the end it's too much work, I'd rather risk my life than walk that far, so I stick with it. I spend my days cursing its existence, which gives me something to do besides stare at cornfields, count the dashed lines on the asphalt and juggle the discarded spark plugs I keep finding on the ground.

Drivers aren't particularly courteous, and as the road narrows I find out just how much my life is worth to them. Not much. I know it would be a real inconvenience, what with all the urgency to get from one cornfield to the next, to have to slow down or nudge back from the edge of the pavement a foot or two to give me room. It is here I encounter the most dangerous driving maneuver I will face on this journey. I walk on the left side of the road, into traffic, as I'm actually required to do by the police, so that I can see drivers coming and get out of the way when they fall asleep or try to hit me on purpose, which is often. This means that I'm blind to the rear. The danger comes when someone decides to pass another car as he's coming up behind me, which means he has to get into my usually empty lane and reduce my 10-12 foot cushion to 2-3 feet, while doing about 80 m.p.h. And I don't see him coming. Obviously, this always happens when there are no cars in my lane, when I relax a bit and don't worry about having to jump off the road to save my life. So when he does this it scares the hell out of me. Twice I literally get blown a few inches off the road, only to be sucked back into traffic immediately after as they pass. My usual good manners go right out the window and my middle finger goes into the air, something I haven't done since the last time I drove to work on the freeway back home. Doesn't matter, they never stop, which is good because I don't know what I'd do if they did.

I've crossed a time zone, so if I break a leg tomorrow at least I can say I walked across a time zone. I'm about five days from the Mississippi River, another milestone. Illinois looks like Indiana, which looked like Ohio. I don't know why I keep expecting dramatic changes in scenery whenever I cross a state line. There are more towns here, more people, so camping is getting a little harder again. I sleep in fields mostly, cemeteries when I can find them, and on the occasional golf course — an opportunity I relish in a petty, vindictive sort of way. I've always had a hard time respecting golf. It just takes itself too seriously. Listen, if LeBron James can hit a free throw with 20,000 people screaming in his face, Tiger Woods should be able to tap in a putt without throwing a fit when someone sneezes. And don't get me started on the dress code. I figure the least golf can do to make amends is to let me sleep on a fairway every now and again.

I have named the jogger. This was bound to happen. I walk with her all day. We sweat together, we dodge semis together, we throw temper tantrums and tell off old people together. People glare at me, dogs lift their legs on her. My long-suffering feet have bonded with her scuffed and balding tires. At night I even sleep with her, so I better know her name when she wakes up in the morning.

We look like a circus act, Sideshow Bob and his trained seal . . . but what's that seal called? As of now she is called BJ. I know, stop snickering — BJ stands for "Baby Jogger." Just seemed natural. A good buddy name, a good name for a traveling partner.

Outside Montrose, BJ and I secure the most miserable camping spot of the trip — even worse than the muddy culvert — when we're forced into a swamp because there are houses everywhere and there's nowhere else to go. I'm trampling reeds and cattails, trying to flatten a spot big enough to set the tent down. Below is shoe-sucking mud. I'm considering placing it among my all-time worst campsites, but I remember sleeping in a dump next to a pile of rotten cow heads in Mexico, and in Africa I slept in the mud on the side of a jungle road while it pissed rain and cockroaches did wind sprints up my thighs. Yeah, those were worse.

This spot is merely a stinking bog bordered by a railroad on one side and the interstate on the other. Trains, trucks, mosquitoes and ticks all night long. It seemed nice from a distance. Like that girl across the bar after five beers, but get a little closer . . .

The next night Illinois rebounds. I get lost trying to find a campground my GPS has sworn is right here. At the nearest farm house I knock on a door to ask directions. A kindly old woman, looks like Mrs. Claus without the red coat, answers and tells me the camp is closed. I drop my head and look at my shoes, making sad puppy face, sure it will work this time — it always works on kindly old ladies (as long as they don't own campgrounds in Indianapolis).

"Gee, I've walked so far today. Really tired. Feet kinda hurt. Suppose I'll just keep going. Maybe when it gets dark I can find a bush somewhere . . ."

The woman smiles. Says she's the owner of the site, it's just around back, go ahead and camp for free you poor thing, and have a Pepsi for the road. I wander down a one lane gravel path, wondering if I'm going to hell for manipulating sweet old ladies. But I think she knew, and she didn't mind. The path opens onto a beautiful, grassy peninsula jutting into a lake, warm light of evening shining off the water, wind in the leaves, an old broken dock for me to sit on and soak my toes, an overturned rowboat for me to eat my dinner on. I watch the water ripple from fish swimming just beneath the surface, watch leaves drop from the trees and sail away on the lake like tiny boats. Not a soul around. All mine.

Illinois is another sprint, and I'm across it in about nine days. It goes quickly because it's narrow, but also because there's nothing to see. I'm not sure how many more cornfields I can endure before I lose my mind. I like cornfields, I like the sound they make when the wind blows. I like sleeping in them, though some mornings I think I wake up with a contact high from all the pesticides and fertilizers on the ground. But day after day the same. For weeks. For hundreds of miles.

During a cross-country road trip some years ago I saw the greatest cornfield in the world just outside of Alliance, Nebraska. Its name is Carhenge. Carhenge is a scale replica of Stonehenge in England, only instead of gigantic blocks of stone, it's made out of cars. I wandered through it in a light snowstorm, awestruck, past half-buried Fords and Cadillacs, thinking surely that thing back in England must be a second-rate jumble of popsicle sticks compared to this. I asked a local who made it.

"Aliens."

"No, not the one in England. This one. Who made this one?"

"Aliens."

Turns out it was made by an artist as a memorial to his father, who had once lived on the farm where Carhenge now stood. And calling it a cornfield is a bit of a stretch, though there were still a few straggly stalks poking up here and there. It really didn't matter. Carhenge made me proud to be an American. I'm still waiting for Illinois to do the same, but how can it compete? Illinois will just have to live with being the breadbasket of America, ancestral home of corn flakes, Cheerios and Honey Bunches of Oats, breakfast cereals I love almost as much as life itself. In retrospect, that's a pretty good legacy.

Days are still hot. Empty farmland, dying towns and not much else. Flocks of birds sit on power lines and take flight whenever I walk by, gliding in a circle before settling in the same spot once I'm past. I save a dog's life as he runs across the highway in front of traffic to say hello. Christy in Greenup gives me $5. I get interviewed by a newspaper, the only time this happens on the walk, but they never run the story. Must be a million guys walking across America. Walk by Teutopolis High School and the sign out front says "Home of the Wooden Shoes." Not the Panthers. Not the Warriors. Not even the Corn

Huskers. The Wooden Shoes. What does their mascot look like? Can you have a football team with a name like that? Do the kids down the road in Effingham beat them up for it?

The road sits right next to the interstate, but today that's a good thing because the morning is heating up and the massive flow of traffic is generating the only breeze on this still and muggy day. In one minute I count 22 giant trucks on that road, all those resources feeding our enormous, crippled economy.

My sign continues to pay dividends. Two rough-looking guys in a rusty pickup go by, then stop suddenly and back up all the way down the road. They thrust a bottle of Gatorade out the window, saying you need it more than us buddy, and keep on truckin'. Next comes Gene, 74 years old, tells me he's always wanted to do what I'm doing, then gets out, kneels down on the road, takes my hand and asks God to bless me and protect me. At a bridge under construction I run across to beat traffic and all the workers stop to cheer. I raise my arms like Rocky Balboa and keep running.

MISSOURI

I cross the Mississippi. Another milestone, the great river, the dividing line between East and West. People say things are either on this side or that of the Mississippi: best corn east of the Mississippi, prettiest lake this side of the Mississippi, most dangerous road between Boston and the Mississippi. Now here I am right on top of it. Into St. Louis, Gateway to the West. But it still doesn't feel like the west to me.

I walk into downtown and sit beside the river. I sink my toes in the mud and grab a handful of Mississippi clay, squishing it through my fingers. Barges push upstream, driving oblique waves off their bows to the near shore, swamping the banks, driving logs and plastic bottles onto the small sandy beaches that line the river. Giant rats, so big I initially mistake them for beavers, shuffle across rotting piles of flotsam beneath a bridge. The shadow of the famous arch creeps across the water. Like a good tourist I pay the entrance fee and ride to the top, 630 feet, high enough to look down on the buildings and people milling around them like ants.

At the corner of Broadway and Walnut eddies of trash swirl in front of a parking garage. A small plaque says, "Here lie the remains of Pontiac . . ." Pontiac was a chief of the Ottawa tribe, a man who once led a coalition of tribes that stretched across the Midwest to the Gulf of Mexico, and who organized a rebellion against the British in the mid-1700s. Now he lies under a parking garage, or so the plaque claims. One block away, at Busch Stadium, a bunch of guys who were particularly good at hitting a ball with a stick are immortalized with bronze statues.

On the bus everyone looks tired, depressed, beaten. Maybe that's what a long day — a lifetime? — of working and riding the bus home will do to you. In my head I'm screaming: wake up, people! Please wake up. Believe what you want about what comes after, but on earth there is one journey, one shot, a brief instant, a sliver of time before we go back to God, to dust, to ashes. I don't want to be a slave. I want to live.

I'm on the bus home. Do I have a home? Staying with Matt, another friend of a friend who comes through when I least expect it but need it the most. I'm so tired my head is hanging in my hands. I miss my stop. The driver doesn't care, but maybe he can't, maybe there's a rule against letting me out at a red light, maybe it would throw the bus off schedule. So I get off another mile down the street and walk back. A woman with a blond afro and missing teeth walks up to me.

"Can I ask you a question?"

Sure.

"Would you date me?"

Date her? That's a weird question. In my naïve way I assume she's just broken up with her boyfriend and needs to be assured that she's still pretty and desirable. She is neither. But I feel sorry for her, so I guess I'll be a nice guy and lie to her. But before I can say "yes" and get myself into more trouble, she says:

"All I need is $10."

Damn. Now she's grabbing my arm, and soon she's grabbing something else, so I gently fight her off. I realize my pockets are bulging with my wallet and phone, like a flashing neon sign saying "ROB ME." I walk back quickly before the sun gets any lower, wondering how someone gets pushed so far down in the dirt that she'd sell herself for $10.

Tired of cheating death on Route 40, I head northwest from St. Louis to the Missouri River and the Katy Trail. The Katy is a 240-mile trail of crushed limestone that sits atop a section of the old Missouri-Kansas-Texas Railroad (M-K-T, or "Katy," for short) that operated from 1870 to 1986, after which floodwaters irreparably damaged the line and it was abandoned. The trail opened a decade later in 1996. If I like it, I can follow it all the way to Clinton.

I like it. After St. Louis, which is just another giant, sprawling city, at least to me, the Missouri countryside and easy pace of the trail is exactly what I need. I knew nothing of this state before I got here. Many times, after a long, hot day, I'd sit in my tent and stare at a map of America, trying to gauge my progress. And for some reason I was always surprised to see Missouri sitting there, a huge blob of terra incognita between me and that elusive halfway mark somewhere in Kansas. Missouri? How did that thing get there? In Indianapolis I had asked a man what it's like.

"Couple of cities and a lot of rednecks."

My days on the Katy are good ones. There is no motor traffic of any kind, and long sections have no people on them at all. Sometimes I go all day and see no one. In many places tall trees lean over the trail to mesh with those on the other side, creating a shady tunnel that shields me from the sun, which is still sending temperatures up over 100 degrees. I see deer, raccoon, beaver, otter, herons and eagles. Walking sticks, those strange bugs that look exactly like dead twigs — except that they have legs and happen to be alive — crawl slowly across leaf litter and into my shoes whenever I leave them outside the tent. Butterflies land on my shoulders and sit there for so long I almost give them names. Frogs by the dozens bounce out of the way when I approach. One night I hear rustling outside the tent. I shine my light through the screen and come face to face with an armadillo, six inches away. It just stares at me.

Then there's the river. The Missouri, longest in America, 2,341 miles, one of the world's great waterways. I once swayed in a hammock in torrential rain beside the Mekong River in Laos, watching uprooted trees drifting down its center, twisting and kicking up mud as they struck shoals on the bottom, catching in giant whirlpools, lazily floating past overhanging vines and boughs of wild jungle, thinking there is nothing in America that compares. But there is, right here. The Missouri. Here its forested banks are also undeveloped, making them seem wild and untamed. At night there are no lights on the far shore, no lights anywhere. It doesn't flow as much as glide by, as if the entire mass of water were shearing off and sliding away. Giant boils appear out of nowhere, and near the edges are those same whirlpools, 50 feet across, with fallen trees spinning in them like matchsticks.

In quiet lagoons big fish swim just beneath the surface, creating eerie wakes that look like the aquatic signatures of monsters lurking in the depths of the river, like Godzilla just before he rises from the sea to destroy Tokyo. At night I battle through nearly impenetrable forest and brush to camp beside it. Then, if the mosquitoes allow it, I sit and watch until it gets too dark to see. It's near flood stage, moving five to eight miles per hour across its entire half-mile width.

There's been a noticeable rise on the friendliness graph. Through most of New England and into the Midwest it's been a gently undulating line, a few bumps and peaks here and there but fairly steady overall. In Missouri it spikes. Maybe it's just being off the roads and on a trail where people are moving slower, and pushing a jogger isn't seen as a sign of violent mental illness. Maybe they think BJ and I really are on a leisurely stroll down the shaded lane with our imaginary baby. It can't be the sign anymore. My sign only lasted one state — I got too lazy to tie it on every day and just stopped caring if people thought I was crazy. And besides a few notable exceptions, no one took the time to read it. Instead of reading "Walk Across America," they just saw "Give Me Beer and Money." So it's not the sign. I think I'm just less threatening at eye level, fewer knee-jerk conclusions to be drawn by people passing me at five or ten miles an hour instead of at 85. Easier to pull over and talk, too.

One hot day the trees have disappeared and the trail is so white with midday sun I can barely look at it, even with my sunglasses. Beneath the only patch of shade I've seen in several miles, I see a pile of clear plastic bags with food inside — grapes, nuts and a couple of sandwiches. I assume a cyclist has dropped his lunch, but I haven't seen anyone pass me in either direction all morning. A handwritten note lies under the sandwich:

BREAKFAST FOR YOU, FRESH AND CLEAN!
- M. Wolters :)

I hesitate. The royal taster is nowhere to be found and BJ isn't volunteering, so I can't really be sure if it's safe to eat. But it's only been lying there a few minutes near as I can tell. It's still cold from being in an icebox. And M. Wolters just sounds like a nice person. So I dig in. The note wasn't lying; it is delicious. Thank you, M. Wolters. Thank you, Missouri.

That same day I start seeing road signs blasted with buckshot and proper bullets, usually accompanied by discarded beer cans, anywhere the trail intersects with a road. I check the likely angle of fire, and it's pointing straight down the road or right along the trail I'm walking on. The shooters are definitely not concerned with people being in their line of fire. These are not the hunters I heard in the wilds of New England. These are the elusive rednecks I'd been warned about. Beer + firearms + yokels = mayhem.

In the tiny village of Portland I approach to the sound of gunfire. Emerging from the forest, I see three pickup trucks backed up to the river's edge, so close their tailgates are hanging over the low bluff at water's edge. Beer cans — Stag and Busch — litter the grass like flowers blooming in a field. Seven or eight people are lounging on the ground and on the tailgates, drinking and shooting into the river, and clear across it to the far bank. And they're in the middle of town. Houses are directly across the road, with the pub a few steps beyond. I ask what they're shooting at.

"Sticks and thangs."

"What's on the other side of the river?"

"Thought I seen a deer."

"No people over there?"

"Nah."

I consider his answer for a second, thinking it's very possible someone could be hiking, fishing or hunting on the other side. Without really thinking, I say:

"That probably wouldn't go over so well in California."

He takes another shot and spits on the ground.

"This is America, this ain't California."

They invite me to the pub. NASCAR is on the T.V. and everyone is yelling at it. All I see are cars driving in a circle. Again and again. I secretly pray for someone to crash so I can be mildly entertained. But everyone's so fired up already, I'm not sure what they'd do if it actually got exciting. Shoot their guns into the ceiling? Everyone knows the drivers' names, like sports fans anywhere else would know the players on their favorite NFL team. Dale Earnhardt is God, Jesus a close second. His likeness is on posters, on T-shirts, even on napkins. I wonder if he's on wallpaper and underwear too. Number 3 never died in Missouri.

The tent is set up in the field of blooming beer cans. It's hot, probably still in the 90s at 11 o'clock at night. I'm doing my usual thing — sitting in my underwear, sweating. I'd rather just sleep outside on the ground but the mosquitoes and thunderstorms won't allow it. I get up and wade into the river. I want to get naked but they might shoot me for that around here. It's dead quiet except for the gurgle of water swirling around a log snagged in the shallows. Lightning in the distance but too far for thunder. On the mud at the river's bank something is glowing, small specks that look like faint and distant stars. Glowworms, the larval stage of fireflies.

In the middle of the night I sit straight up from a deep sleep. What just happened? Gunshot. Then another. It's 1 a.m. on a Wednesday morning. I peek around the tent flap to see the same man I spoke with earlier, sitting in his truck chugging yet another beer and firing into the darkness across the river.

"Want a beer?" he says.

"Nah, I'm good."

He shrugs his shoulders, empties his can and chucks it in the river. Fires a couple more rounds into the darkness. He waves and drives off.

The trail sticks by the river. I climb to the tops of sheer sandstone cliffs, out of place here, like something misplaced by God when he was building Utah. Indian rock art decorates overhangs and small springs where water leaps from the rock to the river below. On the far shore, somewhere in the forest where the river once ran but no longer does, Lewis and Clark camped in 1804 during their survey of the recently acquired Louisiana Purchase. Daniel Boone also roamed here. When the course of the river snakes and bends back upon itself, the trail leaves its banks and cuts across swaths of open prairie.

One night I make camp on the summit of a low hill with views of grasslands and wooded streams to the northwest. There are grasshoppers everywhere, crawling up my legs and bouncing off my forehead as they scatter in panic with every step I take. The ground is flat but the grass is four feet high. The only thing I can do is fold it down flat to make a spot for the tent, trying to squish as few bugs as possible. I work my way out in a circle, backing up as I go, when I bump into something. A headstone. Very old, so weathered I can no longer make out the writing carved on its face. Then three more, lost in the tall grass. At one point no doubt tended to and cared for by family members, who then died themselves or moved on until these lonely graves were forgotten and lost to the prairie. And what a spectacular place to be lost in. When the world forgets you — and it will, no matter how elaborate your tombstone — what better spot to lie down in than the whispering prairie, with the birds and snakes and grasshoppers, the rustling grass and passing thunderstorms, all that life and energy. Not a bad place to spend eternity.

It takes guts to call yourself a city when all you've got to show for yourself are a dozen buildings, and half of those are shuttered ruins from the 1800s. But that's exactly what Clifton City did. The information display on the trail out front claims this was one of Jesse James' hideouts, though I don't know where he'd hide. Maybe behind that tree over there. Another town that boomed with the railroad 120 years ago, then just moldered away.

Some miles down the trail in Tebbetts, an old farm house has a sign on it: "Katy Trail Shelter." A smaller, handwritten note by the door says, "Key hanging on utility pole beside building." Yep, there it is. I open the door and can't believe my eyes. Beds with mattresses, a refrigerator, a microwave, hot water, showers, a mini-library and air conditioning. Air conditioning! And they just leave it here, unguarded, for use by wandering, baby-jogger-pushing weirdos like myself? I'm so excited I run outside and practically yell at the woman on the porch next door: "If this place were in California it'd be looted and fire-bombed within 24 hours!" She laughs nervously and looks away. I decide to stay. Asking price is $5, just put it in an envelope and mail it in, we trust you. There's no one around, nothing to do except sit on the porch and stare at the telephone pole out front, which I do for about five hours.

Night falls. With each passing minute the house becomes less *Little House on the Prairie* and more *Amityville Horror.* It's old, cavernous and noisy, with rows of empty bunk beds that make it look like the sleeping quarters of a shuttered insane asylum. It creaks and settles through the night. Tree branches scratch the walls outside. I crank the air conditioner all the way up to drown out scary noises, but still I hear things. My imagination takes over.

It's the perfect time for ghost stories.

I once lived in a haunted house. More like a haunted apartment. Didn't know it was haunted initially, and until I found out, the scariest thing in that place was my roommate's back hair. Every time he went to the bathroom he'd shed little black hairs from various parts of his body, until the floor was covered with them. So every night when nature called I went in that same bathroom to do my business, and when I came out some of that hair would stick to my feet. Then it would come back to bed with me. In the morning it looked like a pair of Tibetan yaks had made sweet, passionate love in that bed.

But one day I found out we were not alone in that house — me, my roommate and his back hair. I was working at a physical therapy office at the time, and one of my patients was a nice old French lady named Francine who had a shattered kneecap. During exercises we engaged in idle chit-chat to pass the time. Francine told me she lived in an older part of town and had some oddball neighbors, an elderly couple and their two middle-aged sons who lived together in a broken-down hovel next door. The old man was apparently a pervert who watched Francine's teenage daughter through gaps in the wooden fence, until Francine's husband got mad one day and threw a brick at the fence while the old man was looking through it. The old lady never spoke, nor did the youngest son, who, according to Francine, had fried his brain doing too much acid in high school. The oldest son's stated goal was to wait for his parents to die so he could inherit the house.

"But that's nothing compared to the house across the street," Francine said in a lowered voice. That house had seen much worse. That house had seen murder.

Another family had lived there. A man, a woman, and their only son, who was a young man himself. This being the 70s at the time, everyone was on drugs. Apparently the kid, who had become paranoid from constant, heavy drug use, had convinced himself that communist China was about to launch nuclear warheads straight into downtown Huntington Beach. He implored his parents to build a bomb shelter in the house or out back in the yard. When they refused, he killed them with a hatchet and a screwdriver.

Francine described a few of her other weird neighbors before coming full circle again to the pervert and his brood next door. They lived right across the street from the murder house, she said. Their yard was a mess. Looked like a dump. Had an old rusted pickup truck on the side of the house facing the street. It hadn't moved in 40 years, she said.

"That *is* strange," I said. "I know a family just like that. There's an old pickup truck up on blocks, and every few days they all go out together and sit in it for an hour, just staring out the windows. Weirdest thing I ever saw."

Francine was quiet. Looked at me kind of sideways. Then she smiled. Where did you say you lived again?, she asked.

"I live . . ." The words trailed off. I knew where this was going. Crazy neighbors. Yard that looks like a landfill. Old truck out the back.

I lived across the street from them.

I lived in the murder house.

Things were never the same after that. My roommate's back hair played second fiddle to things that went bump in the night and shadows seen out of the corners of my eyes. My roommate surfed, as did I, but while I was in school trying (and failing) to be responsible, he had no such delusions. He groveled, he scraped, and when he had enough money he'd bail out for months on end chasing waves in the far reaches of the planet. Which meant I was alone in that house. Every time I looked in the bathroom mirror I expected to see a lady with a screwdriver in her ear and an axe in her hand standing behind me. During commercial breaks on *Star Trek* I'd turn around on the couch and stare into the darkened room behind me, where I'd swear I heard something. But there was never anything there.

Until one night. I'd gone to bed. I woke up, checked the clock. Eleven-something at night. Fell asleep. Woke up again sometime after midnight. I kept waking up and looking at my dresser, which had some random things sitting on top, among them an expandable file organizer which held my bills and receipts. I couldn't figure out why I kept looking over there. Then I heard it — a small shuffling noise coming from the dresser, or maybe from the wall. Like fingernails scratching across its surface. Something was moving.

But I was tired. I drifted off. I woke up a third time and looked at the clock. It was just after 2:00 a.m. The same shuffling, scratching noise, coming from the dresser. Were there mice in my drawers? I raised my head slightly and looked at the organizer on top. And just as I did, right at that *very* moment, it slid off the dresser and crashed to the floor. It didn't just fall, it flew. I blinked. My hair stood on end. I looked at the walls to see if blood was oozing out of them. No. Looked at the darkened doorway for signs of angry ghosts with tools and garden implements sticking out of their heads. Nothing. I was terrified, but really, really sleepy. What should I do? Run screaming down the street in my underwear? Hardly. Instead, I did what any rational, level-headed adult would do — I went into fetal position and pulled the covers over my head, waiting for the icy fingers of death to creep under the sheets and drag me off to hell. I fell back asleep.

In the morning I thought I had dreamed it. But the organizer was on the floor. All the way on the other side of the room. Papers everywhere. I tried to explain it away. The organizer *was* leaning over the edge of the dresser. Maybe it didn't fly off at all. Maybe it just fell. But at the exact moment I was staring at it? How did it get to the other side of the room? And what was that shuffling noise?

Nothing else ever happened. Sometime later I moved out, and the haunted apartment was demolished and replaced with something new and beige. That was that. My lone experience with the paranormal — attacked by a flying cardboard organizer.

But here in Tebbetts things are getting interesting. The blasting air conditioner is effectively muffling noises within the room — like, say, the sound of a headless body slowly dragging itself across the floor to my bunk bed. But there are louder sounds coming from the floor above me. Unsettling sounds. Pops and creaks. And shuffling. Oh God, no. Not shuffling.

This isn't working. I'll need a vodka and an exorcist to make it through the night. I have neither. Time for some ghost hunting.

I get up and walk across the floor. I turn on all the lights (because ghosts hate light and are effectively rendered harmless by it — everyone knows that). But the light is out in the stairwell. Of course it is. I click the switch a few times and the sound echoes softly up the stairwell to the waiting darkness. It's a trap, I know it. But I can't turn back.

I take a step and feel a draft to my right, coming from a darkened doorway at the base of the stairs (was it there a second ago?). Looks like a storeroom — perfect for stuffing the dead bodies of travelers past. I take a breath and step inside, slowly feeling my way around with my fingers and inching my toes forward. My hands bump into something cold and metallic — probably a tangle of bloody meat hooks — and it clangs to the floor. I can't see my hand in front of my face. I know I'm making it easy for them, but that's the idea — offer myself up on a platter so they can take me now and get it over with, instead of toying with me all through the night and ruining any chance of getting some sleep.

But they don't take the bait. I guess they want to do this the hard way. I shuffle out of the storeroom and crawl up the stairs to the second floor. A dim light from the house across the street fills the room with a soft, ethereal glow. Two rows of empty bunk beds, indiscernible pictures on the walls and nothing else. I sit down cross-legged in the middle of the floor and close my eyes. More bait. Still they don't take it. I'm pretty disgusted. If they come for me later after all this, I'll be really pissed off.

The floor continues to creak, but up here it doesn't sound like footsteps, it just sounds like the wind. The mysterious shuffling has ceased, and when I step outside to the upper porch I see evidence of the culprits: rat turds. Rats and the wind. Makes sense. I stumble down the stairs, whistling as I go. At the bottom, just to cover my bases, I close the door to the stairway. If I wake up during the night and see it open with the dolls from Rochester standing there, arms outstretched, whispering, "Come play with us . . . ," well, there's still time to run screaming down the street in my underwear.

I spend my nights by the river, sometimes cutting my days short because I know the trail moves inland and I'll have to hop a fence or sleep in a field if I don't end here. In fact, I've added a few extra days to my walk just to be able to follow the river awhile longer. Water — I can't be away from it. The Great Lake in Pennsylvania, this river in the heart of America, they're surrogates for the ocean I grew up next to and can't live without. I don't know how people experience the sea and go back home, content to live a landlocked existence. If I could transport one of these tiny country towns to the central coast of California and be able to make a living there, I'd be the happiest person on Earth. Instead I endure freeways, traffic jams, shopping malls, smog, crowds and parking regulations to have the ocean near so I can jump in it every day. I have a standing rule with friends back home that while I'm out here, a thousand miles and months of walking from the ocean, they can't call and leave messages telling me I'm missing the best days of surfing they've had all year. They ignore me and call anyway. On these days I seek out streams, lakes, ponds and rivers to sleep beside. When I get to the deserts the wind will have to do.

In a convenience store I see a photograph of a man in suspenders holding a giant check, something about the lottery and how he won it, wasn't going to retire but it was nice to have some money in the bank. Sometimes I think the wrong people win the lottery. A guy works at a lawnmower shop for 30 years, then wins $50 million. Reporter asks him what he's going to do now that he's rich, and he says something like, "I'm a simple guy. I think I'll just keep working at the shop and maybe take the missus to Disney World like we always talked about."

No.

You don't win the lottery and keep working at the lawnmower shop, even if you enjoy fixing lawnmowers. And you don't go to Disney World. In fact, you stay away from Florida altogether. You do better. You think bigger. You dream. You go to Africa to see the last snows of Kilimanjaro. You become a philanthropist. Learn to paint. Open a ranch for retired horses. Move to Big Sur. Learn to sail and get lost in the South Pacific. Pay off a friend's mortgage. Throw parties and swing from chandeliers. Ride camels across the steppes of Central Asia. You quit your stinking job and you walk across America.

I make friends with animals. Whether that's because I'm some sort of clueless beast master — an idiot savant with animals — or because I smell like a piece of beef jerky that's been lost behind a seat cushion for the last three months, I'll never know. But they seem to like me. Dogs have followed me for hours. Cats have materialized out of nowhere and curled up outside my tent at night.

I was never a cat person until I met my maybe girlfriend. She has a cat named Cleveland, after President Grover Cleveland, because her best friend had a cat named Nixon, and she thought it would be cool to carry on the tradition of naming cats after dead presidents. But "Cleveland" is a bit unwieldy. Just takes too long to say it. So the cat became Clevers. Then one day I came home to hear my maybe girlfriend calling the cat "Boo-Boo." Boo-Boo? Where did that come from? "It just sounded cute," she answered.

I have another name for that damn cat — Mittens, which is what I swear I'm going to make out of her if she wakes me up one more time at 4:30 in the morning demanding breakfast. But she is undeniably cute. It's her get-out-of-jail-free card, her ace in the hole.

"That cat barfed all over the carpet again."

"But she's so cute!"

"She crapped down the outside of the litter box again."

"But she's so cute!"

And so she is. She lays on her back in the sun with her paws folded over her chest like a baby fur seal. She sits on your lap and purrs. Licks your cheek when you scratch her back. I'll admit it — I miss Boo-Boo.

So I make up for it by finding other Boo-Boos whenever I can, be they feline or canine. Today I meet one, a scruffy dog sitting at a crossroads barking at anything that passes, trying to make friends. I arrive and it begins trotting alongside. Big but friendly, some kind of mutt. I decide it's a boy for no good reason. I try to get rid of him after awhile, for his own good, but he pays no attention to me, just sort of tilts his head when I talk to him. BJ seems to like him, too, and she doesn't usually get on too well with animals. We feed him some beef jerky, which probably isn't helping to get rid of him. And I start calling him "Boo-Boo."

Boo-Boo follows us through the afternoon. He doesn't look homeless — looks well fed, has a shiny coat — and I can't really figure out what he's doing out here by himself. I hope he didn't just run away from home. Seems to know where he's going, if you can get that feeling from a dog. Maybe he thinks he's a cat — wanders around outside all day and only comes home for dinner. BJ wants to keep him but I think she knows the answer.

We come to a country bar where a road dead-ends at the river's edge. There are several pickups out front. I park BJ in the bushes while Boo-Boo runs off to pee on a telephone pole. I get the usual treatment in these out-of-the-way watering holes — people go quiet when I walk in. But they usually start right back up with an offer to join in if I like.

Not this time. I ask the bartender for some food and he mumbles something about onion rings, so I say okay and I'll have a beer as well, because this doesn't strike me as a Diet Coke sort of establishment. A couple of drunks are sitting at the bar, mumbling and nodding my way. I smile and they stare.

I'm already thinking I'll skip the onion rings and head on out, when one of the drunks turns towards me.

"You the guy with the baby stroller?"

"Uh, jogger," I gently correct him. Then quickly: "I'm walking across America."

This usually does the trick. I expect them to lighten up and say good job or that's awesome or something to that effect, but they just keep staring, unsmiling. The one closest to me looks really drunk, lower lip hanging off his jaw, dull eyes, dumb stare. Looks like he's got three living brain cells in his head, two of which are fighting. Which leaves one to make all the decisions.

They mumble to each other and laugh, but it's not nice. I smile back and drain my beer, because it seems like the manly thing to do, and maybe they'll appreciate it and give me a few seconds to leave before starting up again.

"I didn't think girls drank beer."

Great. This is like a bad movie. I get up to walk out and they escalate, something about coon dogs and hunting homosexuals. I walk past and one says to me:

"Where you going now, little girl?"

I'm trying to think of something to say, neutral and non-confrontational to calm the situation, but it comes out wrong:

"Some place I don't have to listen to brain-dead, stupid fucking rednecks."

The drunk nearest me is twitching, like he's about to have a seizure, while the other one stands up and takes a step toward me.

I've never been in a bar fight, because I rarely go to bars and I'm generally a hell of a nice guy. I'm not sure what to do. I realize I just gave them exactly what they were waiting for: a reason. I back out the door as they follow.

Two steps onto the porch I hear a terrifying noise, wild and primal, that freezes me and makes the hair stand up on the back of my neck. I look over my shoulder. It's dark but I can make out a wild animal, looks like a wolf, crouching on the porch ready to attack, ears back, teeth bared, growling, snarling, spit flying from its mouth. It's Boo-Boo.

But Boo-Boo is not looking at me. He's facing the two stupid rednecks, who have frozen in the doorway, eyes bulging out of their heads. I take two careful steps back and Boo-Boo keeps frothing, eyes locked on theirs.

"Take another step and I'll have him rip your balls off."

They take a step — backwards, trying to close the screen door but stumbling and falling over themselves instead. I seize the moment by turning and running like my life depended on it (probably does), sprinting into the bushes as I see a flash of fur flying the other way. I collect BJ and rush down the trail, which by sheer dumb luck goes over a wooden pedestrian bridge into the black forest, with a vehicle barrier barring the way. No way to follow me, unless they want to make it a foot race, which in their fat and drunken condition they would surely lose.

I jog for a good half-hour down the trail, then walk an hour more. No sign of pursuit. I ditch off in a secure spot and check my pants for buckshot, just to be sure. Unscathed. Lucky, really lucky. I make a silent promise to work on my diplomacy skills. I never see the rednecks again, nor Boo-Boo.

In New Franklin a man is mowing a huge lawn. The mower is stirring up all kinds of debris — dirt, twigs, insects — some of which lands on me. I feel a sharp sting and look down at a bee ripping its stinger out into my calf, so I sit down in the middle of the trail to pull it out. The man on the mower stops and introduces himself as Donnie. Nice guy, a bit disheveled, wearing a T-shirt that says "Homeland Security" with a picture of Geronimo and three other Apaches holding rifles. "Have a beer," he says. Sure. "Have some dinner." Sure. "Camp over there." Okay. He rants long and hard about liberals and "left-wingers." I smile and nod. He operates heavy machinery, his wife works the graveyard shift at a factory. She comes over to visit, a big woman.

"When I married her she was just a pretty little thing," he says. "Now she's bigger'n a bathtub."

I'm expecting a right hook to his chin but she just pats him gently on the knee.

"She's my angel," he says.

Love. Beautiful, mysterious, perfect. She gets up and kisses him on the forehead, then gets into her car and drives off to start her shift. He watches her go, silently.

The conversation dies off so I get up to leave. Donnie stares into his beer.

"I'm just an old hillbilly," he says. "I came from this earth and when I die I'll go home to it."

I say goodnight as he stares into the darkness, glassy-eyed, beer cans lining the table, cigarette fading like the last ember of a dying fire.

At Booneville I leave the river. I sit on the bridge awhile, watching sunlight glint off the eddies and boils of the Missouri, saying goodbye to my last big surrogate before the real thing, before the sea, which waits far, far away around the curve of the earth, with all of the Plains, the Rockies and the deserts still in between. From here the river turns northwest to Nebraska, while I go southwest to Kansas, and on home.

All day I've been hearing dire warnings about "The Hill." South of town, as the trail climbs out of the shallow river valley, sits the only hill I will encounter on the Katy Trail, which until now has been almost entirely flat as it followed the slow meanderings of the river. Like every other local landmark around here, this hill has a story behind it. At one time pretty far back, no one seems exactly sure when, a woman's pig was wandering along the tracks when a train appeared up ahead. The pig and the locomotive got into it, and the pig lost. The woman asked for compensation and the railroad laughed at her. So she took the dead pig home and separated out the lard, then came back and greased the tracks with it. Every time a train tried to climb the hill, it would hit the greased spot and spin its wheels. A crew would come out to clean it off, but the next day the tracks would be greased all over again. This went on for awhile until the railway officials finally got tired of it and bought the woman a new pig. The greasing ended, and the hill had a new name — Lard Hill.

Lard Hill turns out to be nothing. How steep could a hill on a railroad be? Two or three percent? And that's what it is, a barely noticeable incline. I think everyone was just pulling my leg.

The Katy Trail ends in Clinton. I've loved her, my favorite part of the journey so far. I set up behind the community center where they let me camp for my favorite price — free — and watch a slow-pitch softball game from my campsite. Two guys know how to play and the rest are rank amateurs. Grounders go between fielders' legs, balls to first base are over-thrown by ten feet and nobody keeps score, thankfully. The pitcher's number is "68 +1." Everyone is laughing.

Tomorrow it's back on the road dodging semis. I'll be losing my shady trees, which is bad because it was 101 today with a heat index of 106. Hotter tomorrow. When the wind blows cold across the high plains of New Mexico, will I miss these days?

DAY 81

MAN KILLED BY CRAZED HOBO'S DEMONIC BABY JOGGER

Lowry City, Missouri *– A hobo and his baby jogger are in custody today after the jogger, in an unprovoked attack, forced an Amish man and his horse into traffic on Highway 13 where they were both killed in a collision with a passing truck. The hobo was seen being led away in handcuffs mumbling, "It was the jogger. The jogger did it."*

The jogger was unavailable for comment.

That's the story you would have read in this morning's paper had yesterday's walk turned out a little differently. First, some history. Horses hate BJ. When I was on the Katy, they'd get skittish a hundred yards out, as soon as we were in their line of sight. I'd have to veer off into the bushes while the riders dismounted and dragged their horses by, eyes white with fear, as if they expected a baby with an AK-47 to burst from BJ's seat spraying bullets and screaming, "Say 'ello to my little friend!" They wouldn't get anywhere near us.

Fast forward to Highway 13. It's a four-lane highway with major traffic, like a freeway. The last place you'd expect to find a moron strolling with a baby. Also the last place you'd expect to find an Amish buggy and horse trotting down that same shoulder with semis roaring by three feet off their outside wheel. But of course, on this day, it's exactly what you find. As they approach I get well off the shoulder, backing up a good ten feet into the bushes so horse and buggy can pass. Predictably, the horse stops and refuses to budge. Then it gets so scared it starts backing up into traffic as Amish man frantically snaps the reins and begins screaming (first time I've seen an Amish man do that). Big rig approaches right on cue, braking so fast I'm afraid it's going to jackknife across the highway. Cars screech and lock up behind it. Highway on both sides comes to a complete halt. Horse sits there for 20 seconds blinking as people shout obscenities and I adopt a "what-did-I-do?" look while pointing at the guy with the beard and funny hat. Horse blinks a few times more, then makes a wide semicircle around us, all the way to the center divider. Amish man glares at me (not the first time I've seen an Amish man do that). I stand there acting as confused as everyone else until the awkward moment passes and traffic resumes.

I'm still meeting good people, even after leaving the Katy. A big truck hauling horses (!) pulls over in heavy traffic and the driver hands me a Gatorade, just because. A lady in a Cadillac stops, gets out in heels and an elegant dress and hugs me. Says that in the aftermath of World War II her mother pushed her all the way across Germany in a stroller. "So you can do it too!"

I come to a long causeway where the highway crosses a reservoir, at which point I was expecting the shoulders to disappear. But they seem to know how to build highways around here, or they just got tired of scraping Amish men and buggies off the pavement. So the shoulders remain, big and beautiful. A dam has backed the lake up into the forest, which died off but left stands of half-submerged, skeletal trees to serve as nesting spots for herons and eagles. The sky is ice blue and hazy, the kind of haze you'd find when wind whips ice crystals into the air on a frozen day in January. The temperature is 104 degrees.

End up in Osceola for the night. Wander through downtown. A ghost town, just like the others. I meet some people sitting on their porch watching their deaf and blind pug bump into things.

"She'll be all right," a man says as the pug's head bounces off a tree trunk.

"She's okay," he says again when she walks into a wall.

120

"It ain't nuthin'," he says a final time as she trips and face-plants on the sidewalk. He walks over and scoops her up in his arms to prevent further damage.

As we're talking a middle-aged man drives up, son of one of the old-timers on the porch, with his extremely drunk, middle-aged girlfriend. "I've had two beers!" she announces. Add a zero to that number and it would be about right. She jumps out of the car and sits down next to me, and I mean right next to me. Tells me she likes me and puts her hand on my knee while her boyfriend watches silently. Everyone laughs, except the boyfriend. She leans in to say something, but she's so drunk her sense of personal space is nonexistent, if it ever existed at all. Her face is three inches from mine; I wish it was three feet. I silently plan an exit strategy in case she tries to kiss me and her boyfriend pops. Everyone is rolling around laughing, except the boyfriend. He finally calls her off, and as she gets up she says "I'm sho embarrashed!" Thirty seconds later she's rubbing his back and nibbling his ear, and I'm wishing they'd just go inside, have sex and be done with it.

The non-drunk couple on the porch offers to show me around, so we drive to a spot where two rivers meet above red sandstone cliffs. A massive aerie sits in a dead tree straight across — how many generations of eagles were born and raised there? Unbroken forest beyond. In deep pools swim fish six feet long. The ground is littered with "Indian beads" — fossilized crinoids, marine animals related to starfish and sand dollars. Also called rock cheerios or stone doughnuts. The indians used to string them together to make jewelry. Apparently, they're so abundant they've been declared the state fossil of Missouri. Didn't know they had state fossils. The woman collects a few and gives them to me. "Make your girlfriend a necklace."

West on Route 54. Missouri looks like a golf course whose gardeners have gone on strike — scattered trees, ponds and low hills, but the lawn is a little brown, like it needs watering and mowing. A baby deer is frozen in the grass right off the road; I don't see it until I'm nearly on top of it. It leaps up, bounds once and turns to look at me, quivering. It's the smallest deer I've ever seen, a real-life Bambi. I could cradle it in my arms. Another leap and it disappears into the forest.

I've been sweating for two and a half months. Each day I grab a newspaper to look at the color-coded weather map, where a huge red circle (red means over 100 degrees), an eye of fire, has been sitting over Kansas all summer. I departed from the East Coast for a reason, instead of just walking out my door in California and going the opposite way — because I wanted to miss the western deserts in the summer. But the heat and humidity of the Midwest seem little better, and I picked a bad summer to try this. Headlines talk about the hottest and driest season in decades. Corn shrivels on the stalk, and hay for cattle and horses has to be imported from Canada because none can grow this year in Texas, Oklahoma and Kansas.

But just now, just in time, the red eye blinks. I'm two days from Kansas when a front moves in, like it has dozens of times before on my journey. But instead of a line of simmering, isolated thunderstorms, this rain is sustained, and it trails a mass of cool air behind it. Today is 25 degrees cooler than yesterday.

I'm moving faster, my feet are lighter. Even BJ's usual stubborn and curmudgeonly ways have softened; she rolls along with little complaint. And she didn't even try to kill anyone today.

The road is straight but hilly, long rises and falls, and I'm wondering how long this will last when I crest a final hill. And there they are — the Great Plains. Wind picks up, my hat keeps blowing off. Cattle pastures replace farms. The forests vanish.

I pass cattle grazing in a field and they jog toward me like giant puppies expecting a treat. I've seen this many times before, but, being a city person, it still baffles me. When I walk by, they raise their heads to stare. One or two walk in my direction. Several more fall in behind. Soon they break into a trot and the whole herd follows. Then for no apparent reason they stop, stare for a moment, and sprint the other way at a full gallop. This happens several times during the day. What are they afraid of? Me? BJ? Have they been talking to the horses?

Roll into El Dorado Springs, where they say "El Do-RAY-do" instead of "El Do-RAH-do." Why?

"Because that's what it's called," a local informs me.

But I don't think the Mexicans would say it that way, I say.

"Because they live in Mexico," he replies.

I see my reflection in a window. I look ridiculous. The jogger just looks so . . . unmanly. Maybe I should paint naked ladies on the sides or mount a flame thrower on it or something. Give it a couple of tattoos. Some camouflage. All I can do is tell myself it takes a certain kind of courage to go out each day knowing you look like a goofball. But that really doesn't make me feel any better.

KANSAS

I've been waiting for Kansas. All those days in the east, crossing the Mississippi, through Missouri, and still nothing felt "west." Here, finally, it does. At the border it looks the same as Missouri, but it feels different. Somewhere in these next few days I will be halfway home. I raise my arms in the air. Do a little dance. Shake my butt a little. A pickup truck honks as it passes from the rear. I shake my butt again.

I see my first cactus and hear my first coyotes, iconic signatures of the West. People here call them "coy-yoots." Like everywhere, they're considered vermin, shot like gophers whenever people see them around town. I talk to a tiny young woman behind the counter at a Subway sandwich shop — who by the way supports her husband and two kids on that salary, guess you can do that in Kansas — and she tells me she just shot two of them the other day when they got too close to the swing set in her backyard.

I happen to love coyotes. They're one of the more impressive animals I've seen — a predator of that size able to adapt and thrive in a totally degraded environment. Back home they live in drainage canals and pipes in the middle of the city, thirty miles or more from open country, occasionally making snacks out of housecats and poodles. This, of course, gets people up in arms. Letters appear in the newspaper demanding action — put out bear traps, electrify fences, plant some land mines and have the police spit out the donuts, get off their duffs and shoot the damn things on sight.

My feelings are somewhat different. I believe entire subdivisions should be leveled and cleared to give coyotes a place to roam freely. Humans will be admitted under the condition that they bring an annoying poodle or housecat with them upon entry, and that said poodle or housecat does not leave when the tour is over. Nothing so barbaric as tying them to a stake slathered in barbecue sauce. Just take them off leash and wave goodbye ("Godspeed, Mr. Cuddles!") as they bounce off excitedly into the brush toward adventure and heavenly slumber as nature runs its course. Circle of life.

At a diner I receive a suggestion from a trucker on how to make myself and the jogger look a little less "Mary Poppins with a Tan" and more "Quiet Rebel Women Adore and Men Want to be Like." We agree the flame thrower might be a bit much. He suggests a gun rack, with a freshly shot deer thrown over the front for good measure. Might need to change that out frequently, though.

I don't sleep much on the road. Maybe three to five hours a night. I take a rest day in Fort Scott, holing up in another crap motel. Many of these older places are owned or managed by people from countries in which bargaining is the norm, so it's okay to haggle when discussing the room price. I have never been really good at it despite having had plenty of practice during previous travels. And at this point my manners and etiquette have gone out the window. Especially when I know I'm being ripped off.

"$50 for the night, sir, plus tax," says the manager. I look around. The place is a dump. It hasn't been painted in 30 years. Cats are sleeping on an abandoned recliner in the corner of the parking lot. And it's empty. I'm his only shot at making a buck tonight. We both know it. Advantage, me.

"You've got to do better."

"For you, my friend, $45."

I act offended.

"$39!" he announces dramatically. His wife clucks disapprovingly, as if her dear, naïve husband is being taken advantage of by a slick con man.

"$39 final price!" she barks over his shoulder.

I say goodbye and walk away.

"No! Please! $35!"

I keep walking.

"My friend, you tell me good price!" he says in desperation. "What is good price for you?"

"I'll give you $30 even, and I'm being generous."

"$30 plus tax!" says his wife in a hurt voice.

"Deal."

It's worth $20, but I'm tired. Someone spilled something on the carpet and the door has been left open to let it dry. Now there are so many flies inside they're practically crashing into each other, like planes in a dogfight. I return to the office to ask for a swatter.

"That will be one dollar, sir . . . ."

Fort Scott is a nice little town, at least when there's not a blizzard moving through or it's not 105 degrees out. I could see myself living in a place like this if it weren't a thousand miles from the ocean. The tallest thing in town by about six or seven stories is an abandoned grain elevator. Most towns have them, shuttered years ago when the railroad stopped operating. This one has been closed for as long as anyone can remember. The nice lady at the library says that in her 50 years of living here it's never been open. So what are they going to do with it?

"Wait for it to fall over."

A cost-effective if somewhat unsafe strategy. I walk around its base, secretly wanting to climb up into it. I've always had a fascination with old decrepit things, probably because there are so few of them in the gleaming, antiseptic environs of Orange County, where I live. There used to be an old one-story ranch house with a look-out tower back home, formerly owned by one of the local land barons, or so I was told. At just over a hundred years, it was one of the oldest structures left in a city of oceanfront hotels and gated communities. From its perch atop a low hill, it would at one point have commanded an ocean view of 20 miles to the north, west and south. Now it was a relic, its tower peeking out intriguingly, like a periscope, from wildly overgrown shrubbery and a once-stately grove of pine trees.

One group of citizens wanted it preserved and another wanted it razed so a developer could build a condominium complex. I drove past it every week, until one day I couldn't take it any longer. I snuck in through one of the many holes in the rusted fence, ostensibly to shoot an ill-conceived school photography project involving doll heads and some other stupidity. I really just wanted to be Indiana Jones. The front door was kicked in. Inside, furniture lay in smashed heaps and framed paintings hung in ribbons and shreds. Graffiti covered the walls and ceiling. A blackened hallway turned off from the entranceway, darkness increasing in gloomy increments the farther it stretched. I grabbed a broken two-by-four with nails sticking out of it and crept down the hallway, a slope-headed Neanderthal with a crude mace, bumbling into the lair of the cave bear. Pitch-black doorways yawned like mouths waiting to swallow the next club-wielding idiot who blundered in. At the end, in near-total darkness, the hallway opened into a large space which I took to be a ballroom or, at the very least, the grand main room of the house. Weak slivers of light filtered through gaps in the boarded-up windows, enough to make out a ruined chandelier swaying perceptibly from the ceiling. Why is it swaying . . . ?

I heard something move in the corner, followed by a drawn-out growl or groan. I froze for a second, then chucked my two-by-four as hard as I could in the direction of the noise and ran for it, tripping over a broken chair and slamming into walls, listening for sounds of pursuit as I went. With a final lurch I was out the door and down the hill, hurdling bushes and broken fences, nearly shattering my kneecap on a hidden fire hydrant. I never found out what growled at me, most likely a homeless person semi-passed out in the corner. I hope my club never found its mark. A few months later the whole place mysteriously burned to the ground, the hoped-for condo complex taking its place soon thereafter.

So I have some reservations about the silo. The angel on my right shoulder is whispering, "Give it a miss," while the devil on my left is screaming "Go, go, go!" The angel wins out, but not because of any good sense on my part. There are simply no easy access points available without me kicking in one of the plywood-covered windows, and I'm not about to add vandalism to that trespassing charge when the police come.

I am moderately impressed with the sidewalks in this town, because someone has actually built new ones in the last half-century, a departure from the norm. That's one thing that has surprised me on this journey — the level of decay in virtually every little town I've gone through. Homes, town squares, walkways, all ignored and falling apart. At some point there was enough money to build sidewalks, but most of them literally have not been touched in 50, 60, or 70 years. They look like they've endured a 9.0 earthquake and a war or two — just a jumbled, shattered mess of concrete that in some places has been so completely overgrown by grass you can no longer tell it's even there. At my childhood home in California we had a next-door neighbor who sued the city and won, because she hurt her back tripping on a crack in the sidewalk that had been caused by a tree root. In Middle America the sidewalks would have killed and eaten her the moment she stepped off her porch.

DAY 89

Before the dawn everything is pale and grey. Grey road, grey sky, grey fields. Sparrows sit on power lines in silence, geese fly overhead. Sunrise turns the grass to gold, wild sunflowers nod in the breeze. Dragonflies hang in the air above the road. As it gets hotter, cows and horses take shelter under trees. Reeking cattle trucks lumber up the highway like elephants in a circus line, engines screaming as they pass. Dust devils spring from the loose dirt of farm roads and spin into fields of harvested corn, surprising the birds feasting on leftovers. Cicadas buzz in the bushes. In the afternoon the breeze picks up and moves over the grass in rippling waves, exactly like waves on the ocean. Horseflies land on my arms but get blown away by the wind. Cottony clouds drift in from the north, sometimes forming thunderheads, sometimes not. In the evening the wind drops; electrical storms hover silently in the distance. I lay my head on my pack and fall asleep. These are my days.

DAY 90

I'm sitting in a McDonald's in Iola. A man walks up and tells me he once died for six minutes, and while he was dead angels talked to him. Now at church he speaks in tongues. Says he wishes he'd stayed dead, the world's so screwed up.

"What do you think about that?" he asks me.

"Wow." What am I supposed to say?

"Do you believe in God?" he asks.

"Sometimes."

"Sometimes? Either you do or you don't. Which is it?"

"When I see something beautiful I think there might be a God. When I see something ugly I'm not sure."

"God puts the ugliness there to teach us a lesson."

I have conversations like this all the time, sometimes every other day. People have stopped their cars on the side of the road, taken my hand, dropped to their knees on the scorching black asphalt to ask God to find me, protect me, save me. I am handed business cards at least once a week, on one side a solemn Jesus (occasionally a smiling Jesus), on the other a Bible verse with a line at the bottom saying "Date of my salvation," to be filled in by me when the moment miraculously arrives. Waitresses in diners say "God bless you," instead of thanks when they pick up the tip. People roll down their windows and scream, "Jesus loves you!" and though half the time it's lost in that hot prairie wind I always know what they're saying. I never turn down an offer to pray for me, which I get often. I love that they care enough to do it. And at these times it doesn't matter that I only see God in the forest, in the flight of hummingbirds, in the sea, but never in a church. Sharing their faith gives them joy, gives them a purpose. To turn it down would be an insult.

But this guy is annoying. His face is flushed and pink with agitation, his tone confrontational and preachy. His religion is with me or against me. He's breathing hard, like he's gearing up for a fight. Okay, I guess I'll give him one.

"There's no good lesson in people killing each other. There's no lesson in watching a child die from cancer. The price is too high. Have God send me a memo instead."

His eyes bulge noticeably, like ping pong balls, and I think if I say just the right thing they might pop out of his head.

"Who do you think you are?!" he yells.

"I'm an idiot lost in the wilderness."

"You'll be cast into the fire!"

"I'll bring marshmallows."

He throws up his hands and storms out. I finish my Egg McMuffin. So begins another day in Kansas.

The police stop every day now because people keep calling in about the maniac walking down "the middle of the road." In some of the larger counties, the ones I can't walk across in one day, I'll see the same sheriff multiple times and even get to know his name. He'll bring me something to drink, or he'll just stop to say hello. And if he doesn't stop, he'll honk and wave. Then he'll warn the sheriff in the next county that I'm on my way, and they'd better get ready for people to call in about the crazy homeless man. But it never works. The next sheriff stops anyway, always polite, always nice. "California!" he says when he sees my driver's license. "That explains it . . ."

In Yates Center a sign says "Hay Capital of the World," and right in front of it another one says "Meth Watch." The city campground is a barren, windswept patch of dying grass on the edge of town. As usual I'm the only one here, doesn't look like anyone's been here for weeks. But it's free, the sign even says so.

Another luxury in the park across the street: a toilet block with doors on the stalls. One of those little things you take for granted, never realizing the essential value of it until it's gone. Or until your thighs have grown a couple of inches from too much time spent hovering in fields and ditches. I settle in for long, blissful minutes.

Still a while till sundown; got some time to kill. So I take a walk. Some kids are playing softball in the park and they ask

135

me to pitch for them. Dogs lie in the street, like speed bumps, until they hear kibble being poured into their bowls, at which point they run to the porch, scarf it down in seconds, then return to the middle of the street to tempt fate and get some shut-eye. People sit outside the country store and swat flies. Church bells ring. A mural on a wall shows a mountain of hay bales with the Stars and Stripes fluttering above it. Small town America.

Beyond the town there is nothing. A sign says "Experience the Flint Hills," but I can't tell if I'm experiencing them because there's nothing here. It's completely flat. A few miles later a barely perceptible swell appears, gentle undulations of earth and grass, like a billowing sheet settling back to the ground. And that emptiness. Huge expanses of waving grass broken only by a weather-beaten tree or abandoned homestead sinking back into the prairie. I walk, listen to the wind and watch thunderheads boil in the sky.

Another spike on the hospitality graph, this one off the chart. The people in Kansas are the friendliest in America. I can't go a day without eight or nine or a dozen of them stopping to check on me, asking if I'm okay, offering a place to stay, handing over a beer or a tube sock with a couple of 7-Ups inside. What you see is what you get out here, and I see honesty and goodness and generosity like I've found nowhere else in America.

So it is with some surprise that I come to the Deer Grove RV Park in El Dorado — sorry, I meant "El Do-RAY-doh" — and the owner says, not nicely, that he doesn't allow tent camping. I've done 30 miles into a searing headwind, like walking into a blow dryer all day. He doesn't care. What about that patch of grass over there?

"I said I don't take tents."

Says I can go into town and try my luck, doesn't much care what I do. Says it's only three miles. Actually, it's six miles away, two more hours of walking. I pass miles of beautiful campsites fenced off with barbed wire and menacing signs because there's a prison on the hill. The whole area seems to be a buffer zone that gives them room to shoot if someone escapes. Another money-draining motel is my only option, and in my weakened condition my bargaining skills will be of little use.

But I knew I'd have days like this, that sooner or later I'd meet someone unfriendly, and I haven't met many so it's okay. And tonight I'll walk to the Dairy Queen and order a Chocolate Extreme Blizzard. I'll watch the lightning show. I'll sit on a real toilet seat again and fall asleep in a real bed. And tomorrow it'll cool down, and I'll walk beside the swaying grass, and when I win the lottery I'll turn that RV park into a landfill, and everything will be right with the world again.

I don't miss big cities. In fact, as I've ranted numerous times already, I hate big cities, for all the reasons I've already ranted about. I don't know if Wichita qualifies as big, but it has 625,000 people living in and around it. That's about 624,000 too many. So I give it a miss, adding a couple extra days to my journey just to bypass it. But these are good days, big-sky days with endless horizons. Friendly people in rusty, battered pickups with cracked windshields and a cattle dog in the passenger seat stop to check up on me. I ditch off the pavement onto dirt roads — at the suggestion of Ron and Ann, who feed me dinner, beer and ice cream and let me camp in their backyard — and I walk all day through fields and open prairie. I see no one. When planning this trip, this is what I'd imagined, hiking along dusty back roads through the soul of America. And here I am.

On the porch outside a weathered farmhouse I meet a couple who have been married nearly 70 years. Swinging gently on a bench, holding hands, listening to the birds, dangling their feet. He's humming softly to her, she's resting her head on his shoulder. A lifetime ago they were right here, doing the same thing. Souls woven so tightly together you can't tell where one ends and the other begins. I think when one passes the other will go quickly, very quickly, because for one to live alone is not to live at all. The face of love is worn and gray, and very beautiful, and it's smiling out from a porch near Burrton, Kansas.

It's the coldest day since Maine. High around 53 with a cold wind. Two days ago it was over 100. I'm in my shorts and T-shirt. The sky is dark and threatening all day. I bust out Blue Hefty, my formerly trusty rain parka, but with the pack no longer on my back there's too much material flapping in the wind. So instead of looking like a walking trash bag, I look like a giant blue octopus, tentacles waving at wide-eyed children with noses pressed against the windows of passing cars, parents thinking, "Who is that mysterious weirdo?"

The smashed turtles are back. All through New England I saw them. Then came dead groundhogs, then shattered armadillos in Missouri. Now back to turtles. These must live in the fields, as I don't see any obvious water sources close to the road. I save a couple by turning them around or walking them across the road, but if I look back a minute later, I'll usually see a little black lump inching across the asphalt right where I left the one I'd just "saved." Is it instinct? Suicide? Hot female turtles waiting for action on the other side? Why did the turtle cross the road? I have no idea. But a lot of them don't make it.

In Hutchinson, the basement of Zion Lutheran Church has a bike hostel. It's not much, really just two beds in a corner with a curtain drawn across, but it's free. There's no one there, but a note on the door has a phone number to call. When I do, the lady who answers says go round to the mailbox and grab the key, it's sitting right there. Just like that farmhouse in Tebbetts.

And like that house I'm wondering if this place is haunted, because it's old and dark and there's generally not a soul around. Here I go again — I can sleep like a baby in a graveyard but give me an empty church and I see spirits in every corner. Doesn't God chase the ghosts away? When it storms at night I sneak up to the sanctuary to watch lightning flash through stained glass windows. Magic. But even Jesus and Mary look decidedly less friendly at 2 a.m., their shadows cast on the far wall in spastic flashes of light, outlines distorted and twisted by the projection. And the last things I want to see are two tiny silhouettes, arms outstretched, fingers desperately groping for a neck to choke, whispering, "Come play . . ." Never mind. You've heard that enough. But I still think about it.

I walk three miles to the mall to buy a coat. Some kids playing in a yard can't believe I walked all the way from the church and back. "That's a long way!" they say. The Kansas State Fair is in town, and the Fair Quote of the Day in the Hutchinson News comes from a seven-year-old boy watching a calf being born. "Mommy, the baby cow came out of its mom's butt!"

I stop at the barber shop to get a haircut. Frank, the barber, has been cutting hair for at least 40 years, can't remember exactly how long. Is he ever going to retire?

"My exit strategy is cremation," he says.

Frank is a character, one of those people who says exactly what's on his mind and doesn't much care if you like it or not. Talks conspiracy theories with his customers all day. Cusses a lot. I take a seat and tell him what I want.

"Why don't you just shut up and I'll give you what you need," he replies.

I like him instantly. It's obvious real political discourse is impossible with Frank, because within two minutes he's already told me how much he hates liberals and hippies. There's a signed poster of Sarah Palin on the wall, but he suspects the buddy who gave it to him is the one who signed it. He's trying to find an Obama poster the same size to hang upside-down next to it, Mama Grizzly and The Chosen One locked in mortal combat, an opportunity to rile up anyone who walks in the door, depending on where your politics lie. Loves guns, like nearly everyone I've met around here, and keeps a 9 mm in the drawer with his clippers. If people get out of hand he takes it out and lays it on the table; that does the trick. I wonder if that scares customers, but I don't want him to take it out and lay it on the table so I keep quiet. When he's done he says there's no charge, the haircut's on him. Then he says, "I'm kicking your ass out of here and going home," even though it's a half-hour till closing time.

I stay a couple of days in Hutchinson, but as it was in Columbus and Indianapolis, it's dangerous to stop for too long. It's dangerous to get comfortable, because it makes it that much harder to go back out on the road. Even a rootless hobo like me craves security, some form of continuity besides walking all day and groveling for a safe place to sleep every single night. I find myself looking forward to the empty, fenceless deserts, and being able to lie down wherever I want.

The Trails West Motel on the edge of town boasts rooms with "high-speed Internet and free adult movies." If you have one do you really need the other? I pass a rusted pickup truck with an enormous satellite dish in the back, so big it has literally smashed the rear end of the truck onto the ground. "Redneck Storm Chaser" is painted in neat white lettering on its side. I roll 18 miles and rest in a patch of forest surrounded by pasture. A huge butterfly drifts by, then another, then several more. In the tree above there are thousands of them, as many fluttering wings as there are leaves. They are Monarch butterflies, heading home after migrating south to Mexico for the winter. The trip has taken so long that none of them were alive when the migration began. Only these, the grandchildren and great-grandchildren of the ones who first headed south, have come back. How do they know where to go? How do they know where home is? Another one of those things that makes me want to believe in God, if only those pesky un-God-like things like wars and famines and general human misery didn't keep ruining it for me. I decide to have an early day and sit with them through the afternoon, watching as they flash from brilliant orange to black silhouette while fluttering between shafts of sunlight in the deep shadow of the trees.

In the middle of the night other creatures attack. I made the mistake of leaving out a small bag of trash, and I wake up to the sounds of plastic rustling by my head. Mice. Dozens of them. I flash the light and they bounce off in every direction, like popcorn bursting from a pan. Within seconds they bounce right back. The squirrels have a go at my food bag, which is tied up in a tree.

In the morning is the real horror. Thousands of rollie-pollies, or pill bugs, are coating the tent, my shoes and the food bag. Not an insect, but rather a crustacean, like a crab or a lobster, they are indeed scurrying over everything in a very crab-like manner. My backpack is hanging in a tree, but one of the straps is touching the ground, creating a convenient super-highway for them to stream up onto my pack. I shake it and hundreds fall like fruit from a tree. I've never seen so many. They turned a piece of notepaper I left out into Swiss cheese. Are they trying to eat my backpack?

Scenery changes from farmland to pasture, to forest, to something resembling sand dunes, then back to pasture. This isn't the Kansas I was expecting, at least not yet. The butterflies are having a hard go, as passing cars take out five or six of them at a time. A semi parked at a diner is coated in orange goo, flower-petal wings flapping grotesquely on its grille. I stop to pick more rollie-pollies off of BJ — I'll be doing this for several days — and to get something to eat. Meet some cowboys in chaps and dirty hats I saw the other day and they're happy to see me again.

"What are you guys doing today?"

"Chasin' cows."

Stafford, Macksville, Belpre — tiny towns flung across the plains like beads on a prairie blanket, strung together by the ribbon of the highway. Maybe 200 people in each, maybe less. A water tower, a bank, a post office and a library that's open two half-days a week. Main Streets so quiet I could lie down in the middle of them and not be killed for eight or nine minutes. Graffiti on an old brick building says, "Class of '71 Rocks!" Beside it, "'01 Too!" School could be a block away or 50 miles down the road. Not much happens here, and I imagine that's just how people like it.

In another life I could see myself right here. A little house on Sweetgrass Lane. Creaky porch with a hammock out front, legs dangling off the side of it, cat tip-toeing around my bare feet. Soft light of afternoon slanting through leaves of an old maple tree, warming my face, sending shivers down my spine. Listening for thunder as laundry flaps on the clothesline, socks and underwear drifting in lazy arcs with the breeze. Dogs sleeping under the swing set. Fruit ripening on the window sill. A life full of simple, quiet moments, set around the hard labor of trying to make a living in a place so far from anywhere.

East of Kinsley black curtains of rain from the south swallow ridges of dunes one by one before spitting them out into golden sunshine on the other side. I make it to town without getting drenched and hole up in a pizza joint to stuff my face. A call to the Edwards County Sheriff dispatch connects me with Sheriff Bobby, who stops by the pizza place for a chat. Says I can camp in the park on the edge of town, no problem.

Kinsley is one of those "midway" towns, sitting almost exactly in the middle of the country. The park I'm at has a big sign pointing east to New York and west to San Francisco, each 1,561 miles away. Because I had to be crazy and leave from Maine instead of New York, my halfway point was actually somewhere back by the Kansas/Missouri border. But it's nice to have a giant sign validate it anyway.

Sheriff Bobby stops by to visit. He is a photographer as well, and he shows me some work. It's good, really good. Has some photos of violent weather, steamrolling clouds with bursts of lightning and 80 m.p.h. winds. Doesn't have any pictures of tornadoes but he's seen a few. That's one thing I'd halfway hoped to see on this walk — a tornado. But like a lot of things that seem like a good idea while sitting on a sofa in a comfortable house, it's not so much fun when you're out there in the middle of it. And here in Tornado Alley, where towns, bridges and cover of any kind are 30 miles apart, and they just had a tornado warning yesterday, I'm okay with not seeing one.

Sheriff Bobby tells me this county has 3,000 people in it, half of whom live in Kinsley. There's been negative population growth for decades, as everyone bails out for the cities to make a living. People call the sheriff on his personal cell phone, because everyone knows everyone and that's just how they do it. They go 12 or 15 years without a homicide. You can buy a nice, big house with a bit of land around it for less than $30,000.

The Plains I had always imagined show up the next day as the land goes dry and featureless, as if flattened by the weight of those big Kansas skies. The road never curves. I see my first tumbleweeds, though they're still green and not yet tumbling. The frogs of Missouri have been replaced by lizards.

At a trash-strewn rest stop where Route 283 dead-ends into Route 56, a sign says "Camping Permitted." A miracle, the first sign of its kind I've seen — outside of a campground — in three and a half months. But sleep doesn't come easily. Throughout the night trucks compression-brake as they near the intersection, a sound like a giant farting. I wake up every half-hour. I twist and turn. I have a stupid dream. The police are in pursuit for no apparent reason, a whole line of cop cars in a slow-speed chase reminiscent of O.J. and the Bronco, only instead of a Hall of Fame running back it's me and BJ power walking at a brisk three miles per hour. Cops are walking beside their cars, crouching and taking cover behind the open doors of their cruisers. They shoot at me with BBs, which bounce off the back of my head and really hurt, so I return fire, shooting wildly over my shoulder with my own BB gun, hoping I can slow them or at least chip a headlight. Just as I think I might make it, one of the cars speeds forward and swerves for the rear tire of BJ to initiate a pit maneuver. I'm afraid he might run over my foot, so I fall to the ground and give up. End of dream. I wake up in a sweat as the sun rises.

Make it to Dodge City and I feel like shooting something. Anything. But I didn't pack my six-shooters and the law is everywhere, real and imaginary. On Boot Hill a smiley man with a handlebar moustache is dressed like a sheriff from the old west, spurs clicking. I don't feel like talking to him so I pretend I'm on the phone, which is exactly what people in cities do when they want to ignore me. There are a lot of real police around as well. Someone tells me there is gang activity here, which seems strange for a town this size, but I guess you can have those problems anywhere.

On the same streets where Wyatt Earp, Bat Masterson and Doc Holliday shot bad guys, pink tourists with bellies and video cameras now wander from one gift shop to another. Candy-sucking children whine and pull at their parents' arms. Motor homes back up on East Wyatt Earp Boulevard. A billboard says "Get the Heck into Dodge," and another one says "Come visit the Kansas Teachers Hall of Fame." I'm guessing that one doesn't do so well. I sit in the shade licking an ice cream cone, reading a tourist brochure I found in the bathroom which informs me that the words "stiff" (dead guy), "joint" (saloon) and "red light district" originated in this very town.

And that in 1887 Dodge City had one saloon for every 59 residents. That's 17 saloons.

Tomorrow I hit 2,000 miles.

Head south through a devastated landscape, dry and wasted. This summer is one of the driest on record, many places seeing a quarter of the precipitation they usually get. Everything is brown — earth, fields, even the sky, filled with dust. The temperature has gone up into the 90s again. I rest by an abandoned homestead with a caved-in house and a leaning barn. In the far distance, another prairie fire. No, not a fire, just a tractor plowing a field, the wind carrying the soil away like billowing smoke. In half an hour I count 24 dust devils moving across the ruined field out front, one after another.

On the empty plains no one can hear you scream. But I try my best to make them. Out of sheer boredom I'm talking to myself, something I hadn't planned on doing until New Mexico. And I'm singing a lot. It's not pretty. Dogs howl. Birds take flight. Children hide in their mothers' aprons. But it keeps my mind in the right place.

I moo at cows. They stare at me. As I approach they freeze, then take off suddenly and dash into a far corner of the field until fences block their path. There they walk in circles and bump into each other in a confused manner. At night I howl at the coyotes but the coyotes never howl back.

"Yap, yap! Yap yap yap! Yap!"

Oh no.

I'm sleeping in the park in Minneola. Or at least I was sleeping, until someone decided to take their small, rat-like dog for a walk outside my tent an hour before sunrise. Though I generally love animals and often prefer their company to that of people, I've developed a strong dislike for loud, annoying little dogs. They're everywhere. Yapping outside stores when I walk in. Yapping from farmhouse windows and porches. Yapping from the laps of truckers in big rigs. Whenever one makes a bluff charge, acting like they mean business, which of course they don't, I imagine a coyote leaping from a bush in slow motion, snatching the dog in its jaws in mid-air and carrying it off into the prairie, its insistent yaps getting fainter and fainter, until at last there's one final crunch followed by sweet, blissful silence.

Get yourself a real dog or go get a hamster. Don't get something in between.

"Yap yap! Yap!"

I unzip the tent, wearily, to see one of these half-dog, half-gerbil creatures bouncing and barking at me from about three feet away. Barking is actually the wrong word, it sounds more like a squeaky toy trying to communicate. It has bangs hanging over its eyes — what self-respecting dog has *bangs*? — and an ugly, pushed-in nose that makes it look like someone beat me to it and punched it in the face. Is it a Pekingese? I can't tell. All I know is that it's ruining my morning.

"Baby!" a woman calls out. Then more yapping, followed by some cooing from the woman, which just enrages it more.

"Come here, sweetie! Come on honey! Come to Mommy!"

It ignores her and keeps squeaking, then turns around and acts like it's going to pee on the tent. I grab a shoe to chuck at it, but remember I'm a guest here, in a town park, and I don't really want to injure it (not severely, anyway). So I hiss at it, which doesn't work, and then squirt water in its face from my bottle, which does work. It backs up and blinks a few times, stunned. Shakes it head vigorously. It growls, though a purring cat would be louder and more menacing. Then it yaps, yaps again, and bounces off. Where's that coyote when I need it?

This journey is mental, all mental. Actually that's not true. It's spiritual. The spirit carries on when everything else quits. Mind directs the body, spirit directs the mind. At the end of a long day, and sometimes right at the beginning, the feet might say:

"This is ridiculous. We're walking 30 miles a day on broiling pavement, drowning in our own sweat, bruised, blistered and bloody. Even the knees are complaining. For what? So the boss can sit up there sightseeing and sipping Mai-Tais? Forget it — we're stopping."

The mind ponders. What to do? Carrot or stick? Bribery or beat the living hell out of them?

"I'll talk to the boss," it says.

"Hey boss, the boys are getting tired. Working overtime. They need a little break, maybe a day off. What do you think?"

The spirit rages.

"You tell those mutinous freeloaders that if they don't get back to work, pronto, I'm stripping them out of those country-club running shoes and marching their worthless butts down the road in flip-flops! Now get outta here!"

The mind, chastened, retreats downstairs. It relays the message:

"Shut up and keep going."

So the feet do. Until they don't anymore.

Sometimes the workers rebel. They go on strike. And that's how I find myself stuck in Liberal, face down on a dirty mattress in a dirty motel. A knee has gone on strike. If I've learned one thing, it's when to walk through it and when to give it a break. Today we take a break.

And now that I'm not walking I'm bored. We are creatures of habit, the feet, the mind, the spirit and I, and without 30 miles of highway to make before sundown we don't know what to do with ourselves. I lie on the bed and throw peanuts at the ceiling fan, trying to guess where they'll end up. Click the lights on and off. Kill flies. Contemplate my belly button. Put my ear to the wall to listen for interesting noises in the room next door. Nothing. Even my neighbors are boring.

So what do I do? I take a walk, of course, me and my bum knee, wandering the mean streets of Liberal. The dump sits on a hill to the east — actually, I think the hill *is* the dump — its stench wafting over town whenever the wind blows from that direction, as it is today. I pass a house with no windows. Sits on a normal street with normal houses around it, there's a car out front, a dead lawn with a tree, a porch, a foot mat in front of the door, but no windows at all. I try to guess what might go on inside a house like that and conclude it's either a meth lab or a vampire den. I fantasize about wiping out the entire colony with a pack of No. 2 pencils (since there are no wooden stakes lying around). They'd name a street after me for that. Have a parade. I'd get marriage proposals from strange yet attractive women. But I'm short on crucifixes and holy water, and it would take a long time to sharpen all those pencils . . .

Liberal is where white America ends, at least on my route. In the eastern cities I'd walked through black neighborhoods, but all the countryside in between was lily-white. I went 900 miles from Maine to central Ohio before I saw my first Latino. Now in Liberal there are so many brown-skinned people they might almost be the majority. And there are Vietnamese restaurants in town as well. The local paper is describing the town's Burmese community. The melting pot finally comes to the Heartland.

Maybe the town council can promote this diversity to their advantage, because as it stands now their marketing campaign ain't cutting it. Many towns along my route seem to be looking for ways to distinguish themselves, and some of them do a decent job. Meade bills itself "The Dalton Gang Hideout." Plains claims to have the "Widest Main Street in the U.S.A." Liberal, which is probably ten times bigger than the both of them put together, can only come up with "Home of International Pancake Day."

OKLAHOMA

I am in No Man's Land. Figuratively and literally.

First, the figurative. How many times can you say something is empty? Featureless? Take a piece of paper, draw a straight line across its center and hand it to a child with a box of crayons. Have him or her color one half brown and the other half blue. Don't worry if it's messy; scribbling across the line can signify a stubble of dead grass or shimmering waves of heat blurring the horizon. Finish with a yellow blob at the top burning the hell out of everything. Hold out at arm's length. That's the Panhandle.

Now, the literal. This thin strip of land, the "handle" of Oklahoma, was relinquished by Texas in 1850 when it was decreed that lands north of 36°30' latitude would remain free of slavery. Texas, a slave state, was forced to lop off its northernmost tip in order to comply. Nearly uninhabited except for cattle rustlers and other outlaws, and under the jurisdiction of no state for the next 40 years, it was known by the U.S. Government as the Public Land Strip. Everyone else called it No Man's Land. Sometime later it became the handle of Oklahoma.

There's a lot of underwear lying on the road in No Man's Land. Probably fitting then, given the name, that it's mostly women's underwear. It was the same in New England. Don't know what's going on. Maybe women just have more fun on the highways of America. I find an iPod that's still working, but the end is smashed and it can't be recharged. It's full of country music, so I place it back on the road for a semi to run over.

Camp in another rest stop beside the Cimarron River, the River of the Wild Sheep. It's more like the Trickle of the Wild

Sheep but I'm sure it has its days. The toilet is hands-down the worst I've seen in America. Looks like a tar pit, which I guess is what happens when a toilet's been clogged for a week in 100 degree temperatures. I don't want to guess what sort of deadly new microbe is incubating in there, awaiting the first human host to carry it off to the rest of mankind. I'm not volunteering.

It takes me an hour to find a spot for the tent as there are ants everywhere. Tiny ants swarming over here. Gigantic ants marching over there. Back in Pennsylvania I stupidly left food in my tent and walked away from it. When I came back some mystery animal had tried to dig through the side to get in. Now the tent is no longer bug-proofed against really small bugs. So I decide to ruin the big ants by pitching right on top of them. They swarm over the sides, enraged. But they don't get in.

Hooker, Oklahoma. Named for a man, not loose women, though the T-shirts in the store say "ALL MY FRIENDS ARE HOOKERS." Things start off right when I call the police to ask if I can camp in the park, and the voice on the line says, "Well hell, I don't see why not!" The mayor stops by for a chat. Nice guy, says he'll turn off the sprinklers so I don't get rained on tonight. Oklahoma is going great. Then I'm forced to assign a few demerits when some kids in a pickup spin donuts in a field across the street, nearly suffocating me with dust.

BJ sustained an injury while ditching off the shoulder to elude an errant motor home, an all too common occurrence. Now she pulls right. Spend the afternoon fixing her, though I'm not the most mechanically inclined person you'll ever meet. I'm able to do basic maintenance and repairs on my car with a lot of cussing, bloody knuckles and calls to dad. BJ's got three wheels and a handlebar. How hard can it be?

DAY 111

The Guymon City Planning Commission gathers for a meeting . . .

Commissioner Ted, in a 10-gallon cowboy hat, mixing a drink with his finger: "You know what really chafes my pork chops? Big shoulders! I hate 'em!"

Jed, male chauvinist, with boots up on table, blowing smoke rings at the No Smoking sign: "Yeah, I hate it when ladies start lookin' like linebackers . . ."

Secretary Red, so named for her flaming bouffant and penchant for applying cherry lipstick at all hours, just giggles.

Ted: "No, you idiot! On the highway! 54's got ten feet of shoulder comin' into town! Wasted space! Makes that road look fat! Sluggish! Wide, even!"

Jed, staring out the window: "Yeah, ladies let 'emselves go, just get wider and wider . . ."

Red: (giggle!)

Ted: "We need to streamline! Skinny 'er up! Put in some curbs, cinch that road down like my granny's girdle!"

Jed, still staring out the window: "Yeah, skinny . . ."

Just then Ned, the commission's resident doormat, meekly raises his hand at the end of the table.

"Um, what if someone wants to ride a bike into town, or maybe walk? Shouldn't we at least put in sidewalks or somethi—"

He never finishes, because before he can, Ted spits his gin-and-tonic all over Jed, who swallows his cigarette, which startles Red, who scrawls a line of cherry-red lipstick from her mouth to her left ear.

"SIDEWALKS?!" Ted screams. "IN GUYMON?!"

After several seconds of stunned silence, everyone falls to the ground laughing, except Ned. Thereafter, Ned never speaks at a meeting again, Jed and Red elope to Vegas and Ted builds the narrowest, most traffic-clogged entryway — unofficially known as "Granny's Girdle" — this side of Wichita. And, years later, a severely pissed-off hobo and his faithful baby jogger will be forced to detour four miles around the whole mess, the most dangerous stretch of roadway they've seen in two months.

That's the long way of saying Guymon has no sidewalks. In fact, I never see a sidewalk anywhere in town. But as I'm standing by the truck stop trying to decide how to walk down the street, because it's pretty dangerous to do so without those sidewalks, a tiny, blonde-haired woman pulls up in a car. She looks about five feet tall and weighs maybe a hundred pounds. She asks me what I'm doing, so I tell her.

"Tell you what. Go straight down that road and turn right at the big white church. I'm the house right behind it. You're staying with me tonight."

Ten minutes later I'm there. One story, tidy, nice little yard. Like the house Grandma would have. And a grandma she is, but not your everyday, knitting-scarves-in-the-rocking-chair granny. Like so many other people I've met, she starts telling me her life story five minutes after I've walked through the door, and that story sounds like a Hollywood movie. She's done everything. Dealt drugs all over the Panhandle, rode with motorcycle gangs and hung out with "the AB" — the Aryan Brotherhood.

"I was the main attraction in this town for a couple of years," she says.

Talks about planes landing on empty back roads, unloading a shipment of drugs in the middle of the prairie, then taking off while she collected it in her car and drove back into town. Used to provide backup during drug deals. Apparently, "backup" involves wielding a sawed-off shotgun or 9 mm in case things go badly. Tells me about a time two guys with guns burst out the back of a van during a botched deal and she managed to coax them back in with a shotgun, no one getting killed in the process.

I tell her she's lucky she never pulled the trigger or she might be spending the rest of her life in prison. "Yeah, I'd thought about that," she says. As it is, she spent years locked up on drug and weapons violations. Wasn't around to see her youngest daughter grow up. "I put my kids through hell." Now that daughter just finished her own stint in prison, three years for repeat drunk driving, and into rehab at 22.

"I'll be on parole till I'm dead. But I'm the most boring person in town now."

Her arms are covered with scars from old tattoos she's had lasered off. She lives with her grandson, who's in college, and three dogs. Her house is beautiful and immaculate.

"Make yourself at home," she says. She feeds me, lets me shower and gives me a bed for the night. Leaves for work at the slaughterhouse at 6 a.m. and tells me to just lock the door when I leave. Doesn't even know me, leaves me alone in her house with all her possessions.

"I think after all I've been through I'm a pretty good judge of character."

Thanks, Grandma.

Southwest from Guymon with a 40-mile-an-hour tailwind, the only time on the Plains it will blow into my back and not straight into my face. I pass through Goodwell, home to America's cheapest public university, Oklahoma Panhandle State, and to Robert Etbauer, World Champion Saddle Bronc Rider, 1990-91. Texhoma has three gutted motels and the Texhoma Cattle Auction Restaurant. I see my first tarantula.

TEXAS

Sleep on a patch of dirt in Stratford, the "Pheasant Capital of Texas," watching tumbleweeds roll by. Got the okay from Police Chief Joe. "If anyone says anything, just tell 'em Joe said it was alright."

Texas is big, but I only cross a sliver of it. The most impressive thing I see is "Tex," a 20-foot gunslinger mounted to a metal pole in the town of Conlen, population 18, or possibly zero, it's hard to tell. There's not much happening here.

The next day it's 32 miles to Dalhart, center of the Dust Bowl, where "black blizzards" sucked the topsoil from a hundred million acres of the Southern Plains, carrying it off to the East Coast, where the rain turned red with the stolen earth of Kansas, Oklahoma and Texas. Things got so bad the townspeople in Dalhart paid a man named Tex— what else? — to attach explosives to balloons and float them into the sky, where they were detonated in an effort to make it rain. Rita Blanca National Grassland, which I passed earlier in the day, contains many acres of reclaimed Dust Bowl farmland, abandoned and allowed to revert to its natural state.

From here it's 70 miles to the next ghost town, and 90 miles to the next store. I doubt there's a toilet in between either. That usually isn't a problem, but with no trees or bushes of any kind, I might have to get creative.

This is one of those topics people pretend they don't want to know about, when it's really one of the first things on their minds. Women will ask me where I sleep, what I eat and how I "go to the bathroom." Men will ask if I carry a gun, how many women I've slept with along the way and where I "take a dump" (actual words of a teenager just the other day).

There's not much to it. As distances grow, traffic diminishes, until there's nothing out here but a few big rigs, ranchers in pickup trucks and old people in motor homes. Truckers have seen it all and really don't care who's doing what on the side of the road, ranchers pull over to pee all the time, and motor homes I don't care about, because they generally don't care about me, as their crappy driving indicates. I pick my moments — wait for a gap in traffic, check the wind direction and let fly.

Little point in going off the road since there's nowhere to hide anyway and it just wastes valuable time. And there's something liberating about peeing in the middle of a highway; I imagine it's somewhat like sitting in your underwear at work just because it's comfortable, though I haven't tried that yet. I get caught by drivers a few times, but I just wave (with my left hand) and they honk, and everything's alright. Thank God I'm a man — couldn't imagine going through this as a woman. As for that teenager's question, I'll just leave him guessing.

A 30 mph sustained headwind, legions of flies and the smell of a quarter-million cattle crammed into surrounding feed lots have me cursing Texas. Every time someone in an RV tries to run me over, which is often, I'm forced to push BJ off the road into patches of goathead — small, thorny stickers that look like weapons from the Dark Ages. Invariably, we come out with dozens of them sticking into her tires. The only thing that saves her from blowouts are the protective strips lining her inner tubes.

So I spend the day cussing, yelling and crying for my mommy, all of which do no good. The wind keeps blowing and the flies keep massing whenever I take shelter from it. I can't keep my hat on, so I tie a bandana around my head, wondering if it makes me look tough or just really homeless. Since it's physically impossible to look tough pushing a baby jogger, I'll assume I look homeless. Plastic bags snap against fence posts. Ribbons of sand snake across the asphalt, hissing against my ankles.

Tumbleweeds are everywhere, blowing into BJ, getting obliterated by semis, committing suicide on barbed wire fences. I pass a culvert under the highway, about half the size of a freeway underpass, and it's completely clogged with tumbleweeds. Hundreds of them. I almost feel sorry for them. Classic symbols of the American West. Yet they're not even native to America. Real name is Russian thistle. Texans might shoot you for saying that, but it's the truth. Brought to America by mistake in the 19th century, by Ukranians or Russians, depends on whom you talk to, though it's pretty safe to blame the Russians for just about anything. Better dead than red, except when it comes to tumbleweeds.

I sleep in the lee of a crescent dune. See my first porcupine and dozens of pronghorn, the second-fastest land mammal in the world after the cheetah. Up to a million still roam the western plains, and in the coming days they will be near-constant companions as I cross this desolate corner of

America. I sing to them, badly. Sometimes they run away, sometimes they lift their heads and listen.

What's it like sleeping on train tracks? In one of our more tired analogies we say, "It roared like a freight train." Strong winds, hail on a tin roof, avalanche dropping from the side of a mountain. They all roar like freight trains. But what about the train itself? Everyone knows what a train sounds like. More a question of intensity. What does it sound like from a quarter mile? A hundred yards? How about 15 feet?

I research the topic in Texas, where a railroad follows Route 54 for a couple hundred miles into New Mexico. Decent campsites are scarce; in fact, they're pretty much nonexistent. The plain stretches out in all directions, flat, featureless, empty. If you were to walk out into it at high noon with the sun directly overhead, close your eyes and spin around twice, I doubt you'd find your way back. I go 30 miles between trees. So when I find one it's almost too good to pass up, knowing it's the only shelter or windbreak I'm going to find. There won't be another until tomorrow night, if then.

Two days out of Dalhart with the sun sinking, I see a dark shape on the horizon, mirage-like, a green island in an ocean of yellow and brown. Drawing closer, I see not one tree but an entire grove of them on the north side of the highway, growing in the narrow strip between the road and the railroad tracks. Hallelujah. A hiding place. So much better to relax in shade and cover than to flop out in the open, pretending every motorist isn't staring at me, trying to figure out what I'm doing there, or worse yet, wondering how much money I'm carrying.

The grove is wide and scattered except for one spot right next to the railway, a small cove formed by a line of trees on one side and the slope of the rail bed on the other. I sit on the tracks with my canned spaghetti and dry Top Ramen noodles (a nice crunchy snack, like corn chips), watching the sun set on another blistering day. Looking down at the tracks, I notice a disturbingly high ratio of spikes displaced to those still intact and holding the tracks together. A quick survey rounds up a dozen spikes lying on the ground in a 15-foot span of track, with several heavy metal joints also disengaged and doing a whole lot of nothing. I assume they've been slowly rattled loose by the constant passage of trains.

I haven't seen a train in several hours and assume that this is how it will be through the night. Then a couple hours past sunset the first train approaches. I hear it a long way off, blowing its horn in warning whenever it approaches a dirt road crossing in front of it. Two moderate blasts, one short, then one longer than the rest — medium, medium, short, long. Always the same sequence. The night goes silent again for a few seconds. Then a faint rumble, growing steadily as it gets closer, until about ten seconds out the ground starts to tremble with the weight of 20,000 rolling tons, shaking loose the ridges of windblown dust that were clinging to the sides of the tent. As the trembling increases, heavier things dislodge, twigs and insects whose silhouettes slide off the sides like tiny sailors abandoning a sinking ship. At this point it's screaming like a . . . hurricane? An avalanche? A freight train?

I scream as loud as I can, because my ears hurt, and no one can hear me anyway. I can't even hear myself. But it's just beginning. What I had failed to notice earlier is the side road 200 yards down the highway, which the trains will cross as well, blowing their warning sequence when they do. The first blast comes right on top of me, rattling my teeth in my head. The engines pass, but the line of cars behind it might take another two minutes. Wheels hit rail joints with loud bangs, and poorly lubricated wheels whine and scream as they approach. Will it ever end?

Yes, finally. The last car passes, rumble and clatter fade into the darkness. Crickets chirp, the tiny silhouettes begin crawling back up the outside of the tent. Night settles.

I lie down, close my eyes, drift off. Now I'm dreaming about trains. Another distant warning, faint clattering growing louder. Wait — where am I? I'm not dreaming. Another engine bears down on me, repeating the same pattern as the first. And it keeps on repeating, *every 12 minutes* through the night. Seems hauling freight is a nocturnal affair in these parts. All I can do is lie down and watch the tiny sailors jump ship, climb back aboard, and jump again, until dawn.

NEW MEXICO

Nara Visa is a town that used to be — used to be a bar, used to be two restaurants, two gas stations, an RV park, two motels, a school and a rest stop. Now there's nothing. Wind swirling in darkened doorways, hissing through broken windows. Tumbleweeds snagging on vintage signs from the 40s, 50s and 60s. The gas pumps are at least 50 years old, collector's items if they were in any kind of decent condition. Classic automobiles and trucks sit rusting in fields and abandoned yards. One yard has a row of old cars in front, including a Ford Model T, with signs painted on the windshields saying, "Get Out," Keep Out," "Don't Get Out Of Your Car" and "Stay Away." I'm definitely not in Kansas anymore.

The one live person I'm able to find is at the post office. Why does this place have a post office? I ask if I can fill my water bottles from the tap in the sink and the woman hesitates, saying, "I don't think the water is any good. It's been sitting in the pipes for so long it's all rusty and smelly. I don't think it's safe." This is America?

Another night spent behind a bush next to the railroad. I've made a truce with the trains, even started to like them, at least during the day. They keep me company, and every time I wave to them they blow their whistles for me. This night I'm less impressed. Another side road crosses the tracks nearby, which means the trains must blow that same miserable warning sequence whenever they approach. It's a repeat of the other night, with a train passing every 12 to 15 minutes, all night long. One stops at 2:00 a.m. right next to the bush I'm camped behind.

No idea why. It spends the next four hours idling about 30 feet away, hissing, rumbling, venting.

So with no sleep, again, I pack it up in the morning. There are dozens of holes around the tent. I was hoping they were mouse holes. Maybe. But when I shake out my shoes — a habit from shaking out scorpions during camping trips in Mexico — I hear a small thud, like a pebble. Hello, tarantula. In my shoe. Then I drop my wet, rolled up rain fly on the ground. Now it's a sand-coated corndog.

Monotonous days. I am Sisyphus, and BJ is my boulder. But instead of rolling her up a mountain for all eternity, I'm pushing her along the edge of a ruler, down a road that never ends, never so much as curves, from dawn till dusk, day after day. Scenery never changes, because there isn't any. I count the stripes in the road. 120. Count the steps I take in a mile. 2,200. Talk to BJ.

"So . . . how you doing?"

I get the silent treatment. Again.

People ask me what I think about. I think about the number of days I've been wearing the same underwear (four? No, five). I think about who would play me in a movie about my life (George Clooney with blond hair). And I think about The Secret of the Universe, which I've discovered and forgotten several times because I never wrote it down.

I don't tell them what I really think about.

I think about what comes after, when this walk comes to an end. About being reinserted into society. My impending demotion to working man, my forced transformation to wind-up toy stuck in the corner. I think about the end of big empty spaces, of rustling cornfields, wind and dust and dead grass, moon and stars at night. The end of dreaming all day. The end of freedom.

How can I be so far down the road and still not know where I'm going?

Tucumcari, New Mexico. At a diner in town, a ketchup-stained placemat with half a hamburger on it sits on a table. It (the paper, not the hamburger) recounts the legend of Tucumcari Mountain, a hat-shaped knob of rock rising to the south just outside town. Paraphrased from the greasy placemat:

Wautonomah, chief of the Apache, was long of tooth but not long for this world. Knowing he would soon die, he set about choosing a successor from his two finest warriors — Tonopah and Tocom, the latter of whom was loved by Kari, daughter of the great chief. The two warriors fought with knives for the right of succession and for the hand of Kari. Tonopah struck first, stabbing Tocom in the heart. Kari, who was watching in secret nearby, rushed to her lover's side and stabbed his rival through the heart, killing Tonopah. In her grief she ended her own life as well, with a knife to the heart. Finally, the great chief came upon the scene and, heartbroken, completed the bloodbath by — you guessed it — sinking a knife into his own chest. Apparently tall cliffs or hanging trees had gone out of fashion. As the great chief died he cried out, "Tocom-Kari!" With the usual bastardization of indigenous place names,

"Tocom-Kari" became Tucumcari, and the mountain, as well as the town, had its name.

Or not. The name might actually mean "Woman's Breast," which seems to be the more accepted explanation and makes sense when you look at the boob-shaped mountain. Did the placemat lie to me? I ask a lady at the post office and she tells me the bloody Apache story was made up by a group of local businessmen to impress dumb tourists like me. I can still hear the placemat laughing . . .

Tucumcari. Home to $17 motel rooms and Route 66 tourist overkill. Murals of James Dean, Marilyn Monroe and Elvis standing next to a cactus or leaning against an old Ford truck. Motels from a bygone era: the Palomino, Buckaroo, Apache and Royal Palacio. More classic signs, in fact sometimes the sign is the only thing left standing, the building long gone.

Time for a joke. Or three.
What did the hat say to the scarf?
You hang around while I go on ahead.
Why did the hamburger go to the gym?
To get bigger buns.
And:
What did the triangle say to the circle?
Your life seems so pointless.

I stole those jokes from my maybe girlfriend, who in turn stole them from the children's section of the Sunday comics. That last one is particularly relevant, because it describes my day perfectly — the day I walk in a big, pointless circle. My tribulation begins as I try to find a way west toward Santa Rosa, since Route 54 has disappeared under an interstate. Depending on whom you talk to, New Mexico may or may not be the only state in America in which it's legal to walk on an interstate. The highway patrol said yes, then changed its mind and said no. Sheriff said no, two police officers and a state trooper said yes. So no one really knows. Guess I'm going to find out. I walk two hours to the highway, then manage only 100 yards up the ramp before a patrolman stops me. No walkers allowed. Cyclists are fine, but no walkers.

"Why is that?" I ask him.

"Don't know. Just is."

I try another option that involves walking 40 minutes farther to the end of the frontage road, where a dirt track continues beside the railway. The track deteriorates into two muddy ruts with knee-high weeds in the middle. Within a few yards it disappears into a mud bog with half-sunken tree trunks and old tires floating on top. Might be a couple of mastodons down there too, it's that big. I test it by shoving BJ in a few inches. She gets stuck up to her axles and refuses to budge. Any way around it? The sides slope up sharply with basketball-size boulders protruding from the ground — totally impassable for a jogger loaded down with food and water. I could try to portage around it, but even that looks suspect. Should I go for it? Live fast, die young, and make a good-looking corpse after I slip and fall in? I daydream for a few minutes, fantasizing about my fossilized skull being the star of third-grade show-and-tell when some kid digs me up with a stick in a hundred thousand years and brings me in to class. Or maybe I'd end up in one of those climate-controlled glass cases at the Smithsonian, with signs in front saying "Tucumcari Man" and "Do not touch glass," grinning at lines of school children brought in on field trips, the stuff of kindergarten nightmares.

I look across the tar pit and see several more bogs beyond it. Forget it. I'm not sacrificing myself for that kid's show-and-tell. Guess I'll have to find another way to become famous. We turn around and head back with our tails between our legs. Five hours later I find myself back where I started, my pointless circle completed.

But, as so often happens, strangers come to the rescue. The owners of a motel on the eastern edge of town offer to take BJ and my gear around the impassable part, to an old gas station where Route 66 reappears from under the interstate. From here the old highway parallels the new, all the way to Santa Rosa.

The Great Plains have ended. For the first time in weeks I have something to look at besides road kill and discarded underwear, as low mesas appear in the distance and shallow red rock canyons drain off the plateau in front of me. They pale in comparison to the great canyons and stone cathedrals found farther west, but they're still impressive after so many miles of nothing. Many adventures I've had in similar country in Utah and Arizona, wandering through twisting canyons full of arches and pinnacles, stumbling across rock art and Anasazi ruins hidden in alcoves high upon towering cliffs.

I'm still following Route 66, now through rolling hills of sagebrush and juniper. Scattered along the route are the ghost towns of Montoya, Newkirk and Cuervo, born with the railroads over a century ago, killed by Interstate 40 when it was laid down literally on top of them. Here and there among the rusting cars and bombed-out buildings, many of them so old they're made from adobe, is a trailer surrounded by junk and trash, sometimes piled as high as the roof. A few are still functional, dumped among the dead buildings like bodies saved from burial when they twitched a little at the cemetery gates. Bits of laundry hanging from a line, or a satellite dish poking from the roof are the only things that mark them as habitable. People mill around like extras from *The Texas Chainsaw Massacre.* I wave to several but they don't wave back.

"Do you speak English?" I ask the nearest one. I really just mumble it to myself, under my breath, because I don't have the guts to say it too loudly and have them hear me, which might lead to me ending up in a stew, or as smoked and dried rations in the bomb shelter out back.

"Do . . . you . . . speak . . . English?"

Nothing.

"Speaka de Engleesh?"

Still nothing.

"¿Habla Ingles?" "Sprechen Sie Englisch?" "Parlez-vous anglais?"

No. Nein. Non.

Everyone standing around in silence, staring. Maybe I'll try grunting or banging on drums next. No one waves, no one smiles, no one raises his hand and says, "Yes! I speaka de Engleesh!"

Now I'm the main attraction. People stand with their hands on their hips, acting like they've just seen a grown man talking to a baby jogger in the middle of the desert. On a side road I try to flag down a woman in a truck with a huge dog beside her to ask about camping somewhere. She never slows down, just turns her head to look at me and blows right past. For a moment I consider clutching my chest and falling to the ground, then wiggling around a little, but watching her drive away from that would have been too disheartening. I keep walking.

Wind howls from its usual direction — straight into my face. I scream into it, yell at it, pout. Sleep in an old mud-brick building with "Cold Beer" painted on the side, only the walls still standing but it provides shelter. In the morning the road leaves the interstate and I see two cars in seven hours. I pass a couple of forgotten cemeteries, trash swirling around headstones with Spanish surnames and simple wooden crosses with nothing on them at all.

The tarantulas are out in force. A big one, about the size of my palm, is marching on the side of the road, just like me. I stop to play with it. I brush its back leg with a finger and it rears up, higher and higher, until it rolls on to its back. Well, that's not very intimidating. It moves so slowly I can't figure out how it catches prey, but I guess when you're ambushing beetles and caterpillars, speed might not be critical. I decide to be brave, or stupid, and direct it up onto my shoe because I think it will make a good picture. But before my camera can click it decides to go exploring, and in a few seconds it has crawled up my ankle and is headed north. I take a twig and gently direct it back down to the ground. It keeps walking like nothing has happened, so I leave it there and trudge ten uneventful miles into Santa Rosa.

In town I get caught out again, nowhere to camp and I'm too tired to find a place, so I crawl into a Budget Inn. In the morning I have itchy red bumps arranged in lines up my arms. Bed bugs.

Beyond Santa Rosa, which sits in a shallow valley full of sinkholes, some of which are flooded with lakes, the road climbs a long rise and the scenery reverts back to nothing. Like Texas, only higher and colder. And without nice Texans in it. I haven't seen a campsite in four hours. It's going to be a rough night. Those same barbed wire fences, with me since New York, still laughing at me, thwarting my camping. At dusk there is a single stunted juniper, the only one in ten miles, straddling the fence 20 feet off the road. Minimal cover, no wind protection, cactus spines and big rocks all over the ground. This is it for tonight.

A couple hours past midnight I wake up and stare at the moon. Something else is staring back at me — six things actually. Heads, floating directly above me. Am I dreaming? After a few blinks I realize they are cattle that wandered over to the fence to watch me as they do so often during the day. I sit up and they immediately stampede into the night.

A couple hours later the heads are back. I wonder what they're thinking. They gather beside the fence to observe me, like a team of surgeons contemplating a patient. I sit up, again, and they bolt in a cloud of dust.

One more time before dawn, there they are. I can see their breath in the cold air. Otherwise they're silent and unmoving. The moon glints off their eyes as they stare at me. But this time I don't get up. I just lie there and stare right back, trying to hypnotize them into revealing their purpose. What do they want? A lullaby? A back scratch? A warm, squishy body to trample? In the morning they've vanished, no sign of them.

Flat, golden grasslands at 6,500 feet, with isolated mesas in the distance. I'm reduced to sleeping in culverts under the road because there's nothing else to provide shelter from the wind, or from transient-killing psychos. I think these culverts are actually passages for cattle to move from one pasture to another without having to cross the road. One end is usually closed off with wire. When it's not, I hear hooves clomping by the tent at night. The bottoms are always strewn with mud and debris from the last rain, so I try to check the forecast each day before settling in. They're not the cleanest of campsites. I have to kick a few petrified turds out of the way to set up the tent, wondering if hantavirus lives in cow shit and not just in mouse droppings. The ceilings are lined with big lumps of dried mud with a hole at the end of each one. Sparrows' nests, dozens of them. They're empty now.

I'm starting a new game called "What's in My Shoe?" If you guessed "centipede," you win. It's a big one, about six inches long, and it's fast. The largest ones in North America live here. They are dangerous to the extent that they can deliver a painful bite, really more of a pinch, using a pair of modified legs that inject venom. What's the attraction to my shoe? A quick check on my smart phone (why is it working out here?) reveals that centipedes "shelter in damp micro-environments." That explains it, but it also means my underwear could be next. I should start bringing my shoes inside at night, but I've developed an unhealthy fascination with wanting to see what kind of horrible monster will fall out of them each morning. Scorpions are up next.

Behind the Willard Cantina a man is fiddling with a giant catapult. That's right, a giant catapult.

"What is that?" I ask him.

"Pumpkin Chucker," he says. "For chucking pumpkins."

"How far can it chuck a pumpkin?"

"About a block," he says, pointing to a street about 50 yards away.

"Could you 'squash' someone with it?"

He ponders that for a second before his face lights up. "For sure," he says, laughing. "That's a good one."

It probably isn't a good one — my maybe girlfriend would have rolled her eyes so hard they might have fallen out of her head — but I appreciate people who laugh at my dumb jokes.

Turns out the Pumpkin Chucker is for a Halloween festival in nearby Estancia. The man fiddling with it introduces himself as "Shag." Why Shag? Because he's really popular with British women?

"Worked with carpet my whole life."

Says he once ran for City Council and only got two votes because no one recognized his real name on the ballot (Santiago). If it said "Shag," he would've won in a landslide.

The road out of Willard climbs to a saddle between two mountains at Moutainair. The change is striking. What had been open grassland becomes forests of juniper and pinyon pines within five minutes of walking. The high plain falls away in descending steps of mesas and crumbling canyons. This is the New Mexico I've been waiting for.

At the bottom, another long alluvial plain stretches from the mountain range into a valley cut by the Rio Grande. More broken, bombed-out homesteads. More snarling dogs chained to posts. More people with their hands on their hips. "You speaka de Engleesh? . . ." A handwritten sign on a broken piece of plywood says "Out There." A perfect description. Then another 20 miles of flat nothing. No cars. Just me and my brain again. Uh-oh.

DAY 127

There is some sort of strange melon that grows by the side of the road where nothing else does. I pick one up and take it with me, tossing it as I go. After 367 tosses a fly crawls up my nose and ruins everything, dashing my dreams of a new world record for melon tossing. Guess it's back to talking to cattle.

So I do. I ask them how the grass tastes, what it's like to be a cow. They raise their heads and stare, then look at each other as if trying to figure out what to do.

"Psst! Bob! That weirdo on the road is talking to us. Don't like that thing he's pushing. Creeps me out. What do you think? Stampede?"

"Dunno. Maybe if we just stand here he'll think we're garden gnomes or Christmas decorations. What do *you* think?"

"Asked you first."

"I'm a herd animal. I don't make decisions."

"And I do?! Hey Stan, what do you think?"

"Maybe we shou—"

"Aaaaaaaaaaaaaaaaaahhhhhhhhhhhhhhhhhhhh!!!!!!!!!"

Then someone sneezes and they all run away in panic.

I camp beside the Rio Grande, fifth-longest river in America. First running water I've seen since eastern Kansas, not counting the Cimarron, which was really just a series of stagnant pools separated by sandbars. But even this river, 1,900 miles long, is only impressive in length, as it's narrower here than many of the tributaries of the Missouri River I crossed along the Katy Trail. Something else I haven't seen since way back then is a mosquito. Now I see thousands. Voracious, blood-sucking little bastards. One of those bottom-of-the-barrel creatures, like ticks, cockroaches, or people who write parking tickets. I'm forced into the tent before sunset and don't leave all night, not even to pee. Wake up many hours before sunrise to the yelping of coyotes, very close, maybe 30 feet. Turn on my headlamp and see eyes glowing in the brush.

I get up. It's cold. Wet. Everything is soaked. The mosquitoes are sluggish; a few are stuck in dew drops and pasted to the sides of the tent. I delight in their misery. Small pools of mist lie in depressions among the reeds. I've never seen anything like them. I run my finger through and they swirl like sediment in water, spinning in little eddies and undertows. Blow a breath on them and they disappear.

I walk through the rest of the night. The road shines dull with starlight. An owl sits at the top of a tree, and as I go by it slowly turns its head all the way around to watch me. I hoot softly. It blinks at me. I pass a lonely house, window glowing with the soft blue light of a television left on all night long. The coyotes are talking to each other again, very far away. The sky glows in the east.

I'm forced back on the interstate for 25 miles. It's the only route; there is no other way. Cars blast by too fast and too close, despite the large shoulder. People going to and from Albuquerque, another city I've managed to miss. Another city with people in a hurry. People with a purpose. People with no time.

A state trooper pulls over, the same type of officer who told me I couldn't walk in Tucumcari. But this one steps out of his car laughing. He looks Asian. I'd guess Vietnamese. But I realize he's probably Native American. Says someone called about a crazy man pushing a baby down the highway. The usual. Never says anything about me walking here. No problem. I see him several more times today and he honks and waves as he drives by.

BJ gets her first flat in over a thousand miles. I'm still a couple of hours from Socorro, but it's easier to just keep rolling than to try to fix it out here. When we get to town it takes three hours to fix. These tires are not like bike tires. They sit so tightly on the rim they're nearly impossible to get on and off. I destroy three tire irons trying. I finally get it done then pass out with a burrito in one hand and a T.V. remote in the other. Tomorrow we climb into the mountains, where we'll be for the next two weeks.

I say goodbye to an old friend — the straw lampshade hat I bought for $5.99 in northern Ohio. My Amish disguise, finally succumbing to the combined effects of blasting semi wakes and raging prairie winds. Its replacement is even more of a bargain, $1.07 in the clearance bin at the dollar store. No style points, but it's effective.

The road climbs steeply into the mountains. A motorist stops to tell me I'm crazy, nobody walks here, but I already know that so I thank him and keep on. Another woman pulls over and hands me a pre-made lunch in a bag, like an MRE, with a card for the rescue mission in Socorro.

"But I'm not homeless," I tell her.

"Of course not, dear," she says gently.

South Baldy Mountain rises like a forested island from the dead brown grass of the high plateau. These are the first pine forests I've seen since New England, though I won't walk through any for a few more days. The road follows the path of least resistance, weaving around the high peaks in long, lazy arcs. The wind still blows, much colder now than in Texas.

I wake up behind a saloon for the third time in two weeks. Not a statement that would make my mother proud. But drinking holes are often the only places open in these small towns, and after a beer or two the owners always let me camp out back. This time it's the Golden Spur Saloon in Magdalena, where the bartender is named Montana.

BJ has another flat; the thorns on the road are eating her alive. I call my dad to see if he can locate a bike shop somewhere down the road. The next one might be in Show Low, 170 miles away. If not, it's another 140 miles beyond that to Phoenix. As soon as I hang up, a guy in a cowboy hat walks up, asks what the problem is, then offers to go back to his ranch to get some of that green goo you pump into inner tubes to plug the holes and keep new ones from happening. Doc Ralston is his name. That's a spectacular name, I say. He nods and smiles.

I trudge across the Plains of San Agustin, a desolate, high-altitude prairie bordered by low mountains studded with gnarled junipers. In the distance are what look like giant satellite dishes — the V.L.A., or Very Large Array, the world's largest radio telescope, consisting of 27 dishes, each weighing over 200 tons. Together they form a single enormous telescope that probes black holes, quasars and anything else that produces radio emissions in our galaxy. They're so big it takes me many hours to reach them after first sighting them that morning.

Each time I look up they're pointed in a different direction, all moving together as one. Presumably if and when little green men decide to say hello, the V.L.A. will be among the first to hear them. I keep waiting for something dramatic to happen — celebratory gunfire from scientists in the command center after first contact, or maybe the appearance of a mother ship — so that many years later I could tell kids gathered around my rocking chair: "I was there!" I saw it happen, when they came down and made it Christmas every day or turned us into pets, whichever the case may be. But nothing happens. My timing is off once again. The massive dishes keep spinning, slowly and silently, pondering the sky.

I spend the day slogging across the high plain, looking ahead to the next pass where a forest of juniper and pine will afford some shelter tonight. In the distance is a silver car, left wheel straddling the white line that separates my meager shoulder from the open road. It drifts further into my path, aiming right for me, coming in fast. What's this moron doing? It doesn't look like he's going to stop so I ditch off into the dirt. I'm not happy. The giant RVs are bad enough, clueless drivers not willing to give me an inch of room, but this guy's malicious. He's playing chicken or trying to make a point. He pulls up and I see a man with silver hair and glasses staring at me from the driver's seat, unsmiling, like he's mad at me for being on the road.

I take a step toward the car to find out what the problem is and he smiles at me, now he's laughing. Is he insane? High on Geritol? Dizzy from the altitude? Wait a minute — do I know this moron?

It's my dad.

My 80-year-old father, who just drove 600 miles one-way to deliver new tires and inner tubes because he knew I was miles from anywhere and had no way of otherwise getting them. He'd hung up the phone after I'd talked to him, told Mom he was taking a road trip, then left the next day to come find me. I had no idea. We could easily have missed each other had I stepped off the road to eat or to pee while he was living out Formula 1 fantasies on the highway (he will return home with not one, but two speeding tickets). I want to spend the day with him, but we're in the middle of nowhere and there's no place for him to stay, and he needs to get back home. We change the tire. I spend about an hour with him, then he's back in the car and off, driving all the way back to California.

I think about how hard it must be for my parents, the difficulty of having a restless, wandering spirit for a son. A son who didn't become a doctor, or a lawyer, who didn't choose something left-brained and lucrative, but rather chased after his dreams until they led him into a corner. I watch his car speed away, visible for a long time on the flat, golden Plains of San Agustin, until it's just a glint on the highway. I wonder if I've done okay. I wonder if I've made them proud.

"You got a gun?" a man in a rusty truck asks me as he pulls off the road.

"Nah."

"Get one. Damn government released wolves in this area, now they're all over the place. Few weeks ago we had a whole bunch of Boy Scouts stuck in a tree, about 18 of 'em. Been there for two days, wolves circling below."

"Must have been a big tree."

"It was."

I cross the Continental Divide. 7,796 feet, my highest point. Not very high, but that's why I chose this place, to avoid the worst of the winter storms already hitting the mountains to the north. This is my compromise. Miss the beauty of the Rockies to improve the odds of me not dying in a blizzard. But it's not like this is a poor substitute. Still rugged, still empty and beautiful. And still high and cold enough to freeze my water bottles at night.

Stop in at the Pie-O-Neer pie shop in Pie Town, stalling over a piece of cherry pie. I'm debating whether to stay at the free campground across the street or bust down the road a few more miles, when Kathy, the owner of the Pie-O-Neer, leans over and whispers a cryptic message:

"You just got the okay to stay at 'The Toaster House.'"

The Toaster House? Apparently, there is an unmarked house in town that serves as a hostel for people hiking the Continental Divide Trail, which crosses the highway just east of town. You either know it or you don't, and the only way to find it is to make friends with the locals and get the okay. I've been under surveillance — apparently a man walking through the wilderness talking to a baby jogger raises red flags, at least initially. But I have passed the test.

Directions scrawled on a napkin lead me to a nondescript house with an arch of welded toasters out front. Other random, out-of-place items — a pay phone and a basketball hoop — are scattered throughout the overgrown yard among pieces of old cars and assorted junk. The door is unlocked. Out the back is a refrigerator stocked with beer, frozen pizzas and microwaveable pot pies. Inside is a spectacular arrangement of bookshelves and nooks stuffed with every conceivable knickknack left behind by hundreds, maybe thousands, of travelers who have come before. And it's got a few people in it, too. A pair of Australians crisscrossing the divide on bikes from Banff to the Mexican border and beyond; Paul, from somewhere in Middle America, riding his bike around the world; Emily, wandering around the southwest on her bike but ending here "because I'm tired and my butt hurts;" and a guy hiking the divide with the trail name "Dr. Feel Good." Trail names are okay I guess, though most seem a bit silly to me. I tell him I'm going to have a hard time referring to a grown man as "Dr. Feel Good."

"Then call me 'The Doctor'."

I just stare at him.

"Call me 'Doc'."

Another traveler, one I'd just missed by a day or two, was called "Money Shot" for his habit of dribbling food and drink all over his face and chest whenever he ate. Apparently he was quite proud of that name until he found out what it meant, by which time it was of course too late. Maybe trail names aren't so stupid after all.

I stay in the Toaster House for two days because it's just too good to pass up. My only regret is never getting to see one of Pie Town's premier attractions, the Stool Bus. The Stool Bus is a truck that sucks out septic tanks, but it looks just like a school bus, complete with smiling brown turds painted to look like school children excitedly staring out the windows. They even have names: Loosey Stool, Skidder, Peanut and Pu-Wee. God bless America. Why has no one ever thought of this before?

Like anywhere with comfort and good people, it's hard to leave this town. Nita, who owns the Toaster House and raised all her children there, says Pie Town is the center of the universe. And she might just be right. It sits at the intersection of a number of hiking and biking trails and attracts people from everywhere, the kind of people you spend a day with and feel like you've known them for a month. As I head out the door I'm sure I'll never see them again, and it makes for a sad morning. But then Paul passes me and we talk a bit. Then he gets a flat up the road so I pass him, then he passes me again after fixing his tire. Nita stops in her car to give me apples, dried peach slices and a hug. Emily and Galen stop in their truck on the way out. The only ones I don't see are the Australians, who are heading south as long as the money holds out, probably until April. So I walk into the wind again, alone, but I manage a smile, thinking that maybe, if we're lucky, at the far end of the road, at the center of the universe, in a little town called Heaven, we'll all meet again to stuff our faces with pie.

Empty road, empty country. High meadows of golden grass studded with isolated juniper. I find a huge owl on the road, it must have just died. Talons like bent nails, death from above, itself killed by a truck or motor home. In the evening I make it to Quemado and get permission to camp at the rodeo grounds about a mile behind town by the cemetery. I set up and go into town for food, a taco plate in a diner, made with those store-bought shells that shatter into pieces with the first bite, filled with ground beef and ketchup. Ketchup? Maybe this sort of thing works in New Mexico, but Old Mexico would throw a fit. Or start a war.

By the time I leave it's pitch black and cold. No moon, stars hidden by cloud. I see eyes glowing with the distant light of the gas station. Horses. More eyes and the sound of paws padding on dirt. Coyotes. They seem to be following me, never seen them do that before. Doesn't concern me. Somewhere near my campsite there's supposed to be an old cemetery with graves dug up by coyotes and other animals, so naturally I decide to look for it in the dark. If this were a horror movie, now would be the time when people in the audience start thinking, "No! You fool! Don't go in there by yourself!" Said fool would then meet his or her gruesome death shortly thereafter. Like that girl who goes skinny-dipping at night in *Jaws*. Or the girl who falls asleep in the canoe and floats out into the lake after Jason hacked everyone to pieces at the end of *Friday the 13th*. Those people who wander into the sewers in *C.H.U.D : Cannibalistic Humanoid Underground Dwellers*. And that fool who stumbles through the desert of New Mexico at night, alone, searching for the cemetery with the dug-up graves. But my movie is anticlimactic. The only dead things I find are some ants I accidentally crush while stomping around in the dark. I make it back to camp as it starts to rain.

The next day, more lonely road. I'm talking to cows, singing at the top of my lungs in a screeching falsetto. The birds are scattering again and I'm sure the dogs would be howling if they were around. I'm belting a bad song by 80s hair band Whitesnake, voted 85th greatest hard rock band of all time in a recent online poll:

Here I go again on my own
Going down the only road I've ever known
Like a drifter I was born to walk alone

The video for that song was famous as well, mainly because it had a beautiful woman in lingerie doing the splits on the hood of a silver Jaguar for no apparent reason, other than that she looked really good doing so. Many years after the fact I had the pleasure of photographing the same woman for a newspaper story, an assignment that ended memorably when she "accidentally" fell into my lap while flirting during the shoot. Twenty-five years ago this would have been a good thing. Now, it was like getting a lap dance from my friend's mom. Nice lady, though. Does a lot of charity work.

I do what's necessary to stave off insanity. I told myself I wouldn't be talking to leprechauns or riding pink unicorns until I got to the deserts, but these long miles, these big skies, this emptiness — they're bumping up my schedule. I'm already singing to the pronghorn and the cattle, howling at the coyotes, talking to an inanimate piece of metal and rubber which I've bestowed with a name and a personality. I want to have visions, revelations. I want to talk to God. And if God doesn't live here then God never was. Just a few more miles, a few more lonely days. I'm ready.

But I'm not on this highway alone. Two things still conspire against me, the bane of my existence from Day One: motor homes and motorcycles. More precisely, unnecessarily large motor homes and unnecessarily loud motorcycles. Despite my obvious bouts of crankiness I'm a very nice guy. I wave to *everyone*. Truckers, ranchers, people in passenger cars, touring motorcyclists — four out of five of them are great, they know how to give me space, and they know how to return a greeting. If the road is empty, which it is most of the time out here, they'll pull all the way over into the opposite lane to safely pass, with a friendly honk or a wave thrown in for good measure. Contrarily, drivers of giant motor homes are almost entirely clueless when it comes to courtesy, etiquette or safety. On the same empty highway they won't give me an extra foot of room, preferring instead to watch me and BJ dive into the sagebrush to save ourselves from certain death. I'm pretty sure they're trying to kill us:

"Doris, look! There's a bum on the road. What in criminy is he doing? Walking on the highway? Well, not while I'm driving on it, he's not. Get the Windex ready, this could be messy."

"Oh, Del, you know he's probably just crazy."

"Serves him right. All those drugs he's been doing. And what in the hell is he pushing? A *baby carriage*? Probably filled with all the things he's stolen. I'll bet he's from California. That's what they do in California, you know. And besides, this highway's for tax-paying Americans like us, not jobless freeloaders. Probably a communist, too. Hand me the phone, I'm calling the police. Great, now he's waving at us. Probably wants money . . ."

So for the 20th time I'm forced off the road for no good reason, mainly because this empty highway is not big enough for Del and Doris — and their rolling building — and me. Standing in the bushes, dumbfounded, arms out at my sides, wondering what could possibly be going through their heads, though I think I just nailed it.

And by the way, the energy you're blowing on that personal cruise ship could power a small village in India.

Then there are the motorcycles. Look, I get motorcycles. I understand the appeal of riding one. Some of those bikes are things of beauty, precision instruments, true works of art. What I don't get is the need to make them four times louder than necessary, and the bad-boy aura that goes with them. Note to everyone: riding an ear-splittingly loud motorcycle does not make you a bad-ass. If you're feeling inadequate, go see a surgeon. Don't buy a Harley, dress up like a leather-clad ninja and blast through the wilds of New Mexico, shattering the silence for miles around. It's like bringing a jackhammer into a church. God won't love you for it. And neither will I.

ARIZONA

I do another little dance at the border, another butt wiggle, though no one is around to honk at me this time. Thirteen states down, two to go. The wind is ferocious, pushing BJ all over the road, the gusts staggering me, like I've been punched in the chest. I see weather coming in as I drop down the last hill into Springerville. At the bottom I look back and the hill is dusted with snow.

A man with five teeth left in his head, loose and dangling like wind chimes, directs me into town. I stop at McDonald's. Two little kids with skateboards under their arms are trying to pay with pennies, hundreds of them spilled onto the counter while the cashier tries to count them. A line is forming, people are getting annoyed, so he starts serving other customers first and the kids can't understand why. When he gets back to them they're 93 cents short. Disaster. I end up sponsoring them and they're ecstatic. Two strawberry sundaes later they walk out smiling.

It rains, then snows through the night. In the morning the world is white and still. The sun hangs in the fog pale and distant, its warmth just a rumor. Stems of frozen grass snap at the slightest touch. I skirt an ancient volcano whose flanks are covered with lava fields and cinder cones. As the day warms the snow retreats up the mountain like a receding tide, the white blanket on the ground replaced by the gold of emerging grass. Beams of sunlight pierce the cloud cover and play across the hills like searchlights.

The endless fences are still with me, even here, but as I climb a high ridge I cross into a corner of national forest. The barbed wire disappears for a few miles. I find a spot beside a perfect, Fuji-like ant hill that mimics the cinder cone rising behind it. The ants are barely moving, slowed by a creeping chill that gets worse as the sun drops. I put on every piece of clothing I've got and climb into my sleeping bag. It's still not enough, but maybe I won't freeze to death. I watch the Milky Way, count shooting stars and wait for the moon to rise behind the volcano.

In the morning my water bottles are frozen solid. Get up and walk — what else can I do? In a convenience store in Vernon a cat is punching a Rottweiler puppy in the face with its paw. The puppy reacts with a frustrated growl, then gets punched again. It lunges, hitting the cat in the chest and body-slamming it on its back like a Mexican wrestler. Good dog. After some hissing and snarling they separate, and it looks like everyone has learned a valuable lesson. Then the cat throws another punch and the whole thing starts over again.

Make it to Show Low and I'm not sure what I think about it. The town sits on the edge of the White Mountain Indian Reservation, and in my ignorance I'd assumed it was named in honor of a great warrior (Chief Show Low?) or an epic fight (The Battle of Show Low?). No, it was named after a poker game. Two bigwigs in town who didn't like each other decided to settle the matter with a card game, the stakes being a sprawling ranch to the winner and a one-way ticket out of town to the loser. Whoever could "show low" would win. A deuce of clubs ended it. Now that's the name of the main drag through town: Deuce of Clubs Drive.

So Show Low is not what I expected. Instead of a picturesque little village with Apache horses tied to hitching posts and tumbleweeds bouncing down dusty country lanes, what I find could be a suburb in any city in America. I load up on food and water and pass on through.

On the other side are towering pine forests. I'm entering another long, lonely stretch, 90 miles through Apache reservations to the next town. Camping is against the law but there doesn't seem to be anyone enforcing it, and despite the fences the trees come right down to the edge of the pavement, affording plenty of cover to duck in and pitch my tent.

I meet three people in four days. Jeremiah is a young Apache walking on the road the opposite way, headed for Show Low, now 50 miles away. Why walking? "Got no car." His story is not a happy one. An uncle who hanged himself, a brother who overdosed and another brother who got drunk and crashed into a tree; they don't know if it was suicide. All this time I think I'm in God's country, but too many people living here kill themselves with ropes and needles and alcohol.

Another day it's a crazy Scot who stops to talk about God, a topic I've become very familiar with. He keeps trying to say "the Lord," but his accent won't let him, so it comes out "Lard," as in, "The Lard giveth, and the Lard taketh away."

"Do ye know the Lard?" he asks.

"I do." (I just say yes at this point. Learned my lesson in Kansas.)

"Then ye've nothing to fear."

The Lard I might be needing as I come to the edge of Salt River Canyon and see the road twisting precariously to the bottom. It's narrow with little shoulder. But this canyon is the most beautiful natural feature I will see on this walk. I've made no effort to seek things out, hoping the small adventures and the people I meet every day will be enough. It's the journey, not the destination. But Salt River Canyon is a sight, offering the kind of natural splendor one might travel out of his way to see. I won't compare it to the Grand Canyon, because nothing compares to that, but it has the same rock, the same detached mesas and pinnacles, the same forests crowning its tops. It's 1,500 feet or so to the bottom, the same amount back up the other side.

Going down is fun. There's not much traffic and from high up I can see vehicles coming a long way off, giving me time to make it around the hairpins with no surprises. Beside the river at the bottom is an abandoned museum and a rest area with the usual broken windows and signs of vandalism. Graffiti of an angry-looking Indian, with "Apache" written beneath it in bleeding red paint, is painted on the walls.

Coming up is not so pleasant. I tell myself it's going to kill me, and when it doesn't, it's not nearly as bad as I thought it was going to be. I take my time around the corners and don't have too many close calls. A road crew at the top gives me water and cheers me on.

On Halloween I build a fire. I've been going mostly without until now, not wanting to draw attention to myself. Here it's okay. There are old sections of highway, very old they seem to me, paralleling the current road. Where they cut into the hillsides they're clogged with bathtub-sized boulders and trees growing straight up through the cracked asphalt. Perfect for wind protection and cover from the main road. So I camp literally in the middle of the old highway, my sleeping bag straddling the double yellow line, still visible beneath decades of pine needles and minor landslides.

Edward Abbey called the scent of burning juniper the sweetest fragrance on the face of the earth. My fire is juniper, mesquite and pine. Not big, just enough to keep me warm and offer a little light for company. The wind blows; shadows of trees sway across the rock walls rising on either side of the roadbed. Fat black stinkbugs crawl up to the fire, hesitate at the edge, then slip and fall in, their bodies cracking and popping seconds later as they are consumed by the fatal, irresistible flame. Bats flitter through the rocks. An owl hoots unseen from a tree nearby, so I hoot and he answers right back. We have a conversation deep into the night. I lie on my back watching the firelight on the treetops until the fire crumbles into hissing coals. The treetops go dark. Wind in the sage, stars spinning overhead.

It's quiet as I cross the reservation. Nothing really happens, which is fine with me. BJ and I roll down a gentle slope. Pine forests thin out the lower we get, until finally they are replaced by juniper and thorn bushes.

I hear rustling off the side of the road. Squinting into the underbrush, I can't quite make it out. Probably just birds poking through leaves and twigs. I get closer and there's more commotion. I stop and look again. The rustling stops. Something is there. Squirrels? Not a bird, not a squirrel. What *is* that? Three little piggies. More like three little boars. And one very big boar. Uh-oh — that's not even a boar. It's a javelina.

A javelina is not a pig at all, but a peccary, an animal in a class of its own. A native of South America, where they live in tropical rainforests, javelinas have slowly been migrating north and only appeared in the American Southwest over the last few hundred years. The name comes from the Spanish word for spear, "javelin," a reference to their long, pointed teeth, which look like sharpened versions of hippo tusks. They're generally poor-sighted and ornery.

Which means they're blind and pissed-off, as I find out. As soon as they sense me, the little ones bolt into the bushes. Then the big one charges right at me. I jump behind BJ — better her than me (chivalry really is dead). The javelina keeps coming. My life passes before my eyes. Really? This is how it ends? Gored and disemboweled by a wannabe pig? But then, without thinking, I do something strange — I growl at it. Low, deep, guttural and primal. Arms outstretched. Veins popping out of my head. Spit flying. I'm not bluffing, and she knows it. I'm not sure if that's the dumbest thing I could have done or the smartest, but the javelina stops about ten feet short, looking confused and slightly alarmed. We stare at each other, it snorting and me growling. I glance at the ground and miraculously, there by my feet, lies a hubcap instead of the usual McDonald's french fry container. I pick it up and prepare to chuck it, imagining a swift kill as my guillotine flies true, lopping off the javelina's head, providing a much-needed ego boost and a week's worth of barbecue in one fell stroke. The javelina makes another mock charge. I growl again. It stops. I reason with it — "Don't do it! Think about the kids!" (Yes, I really say that). It just grunts at me. Stalemate. I'm still clutching my hubcap, but despite my heroic fantasies I'm pretty sure my throw would miss by ten feet, followed soon thereafter by the javelina making a final charge straight into my guts. I make one last bluff of my own, a quick half-lunge toward it followed immediately by me sprinting in the opposite direction. It works. I hear the javelina crashing through the bushes back up the bluff. I live to walk another day.

It's not all wine, women and song on the road, despite what my words might lead you to believe. Some days are just work, a slog to get through them. Some days are dangerous. The walk out of Globe is one of those days. I've been dreading this road for weeks, having heard tales of a highway winding through a gorge, with the deadliest part at the very end — a narrow tunnel just big enough for two semis to squeeze through, and if there's anything else in there when they do, well . . .

A suicide highway. The Highway of Death.

The first grade confirms it. Heavy traffic, no shoulders, blind curves and guardrails with trees growing over the tops to further hide me from drivers speeding around the other way. At the top is a cemetery, so if anything did happen they could just roll me right in. Coincidence? It's already more dangerous than the one in California which nearly killed me and Hanna. I swore I'd never do this again.

It goes on like this for 15 miles. I run to the outside of each curve to improve my odds, because everyone cuts the inside corner. It's deadly enough when people are paying attention. Factor in that some of them are drunk, high, texting or trying to figure out which sort of animal that cloud looks like. Pig? . . . Elephant? . . . Splat!

Halfway through there's a town called Top of the World, which is pretty audacious considering it's not even 5,000 feet up. Outside the trading post & antiques store an old-timer in suspenders, his pants pulled up so high they're nearly to his nipples, is sitting in a lawn chair wheezing and chewing tobacco. He doesn't look so good. He's spitting all over the place, creating a moat of brown saliva around his chair, its mud sticking to the bottoms of his feet and smearing across his pant legs. Doesn't seem to notice or care. Asks me if I'm crazy, then asks me if I'm drunk. I answer no to both questions then ask him if he can watch BJ while I go inside to buy a Coke and some beef jerky. BJ growls softly but I ignore her and walk into the store, hoping to God that when I come out I don't find the old guy floating face-down in the moat with a tire track across the back of his head, BJ whistling innocently to herself. Thankfully he's still kicking. Asks me again if I'm crazy. I ask him what the road ahead is like. He spits into the moat and squints at me.

"Suicide."

But I'm too handsome to die, and this road knows it. I employ my usual strategy — run like hell around the corners and pray there's no one coming the other way — and make it to the dreaded tunnel through the mountain. But right there, at the most dangerous part, the old road that was buried beneath the new one reappears and veers off around the mountain past a gate and a large "No Trespassing" sign. Choosing life, I ignore the sign, trading the Highway of Death for one that probably hasn't seen a car in 50 years. I'm not sure it's even passable, as I try to coax BJ along a nearly disintegrated trail clogged with softball-sized rocks, boulders the size of cars and fully grown trees stabbing up through the tortured asphalt. After a rough start BJ settles down and we roll on through. I can finally exhale, and for the first time I realize how dramatic and beautiful the canyon is, deep and vertical with huge fingers of rock jutting from its flanks and ridge tops.

We enter the desert. I see my first saguaros, the iconic cacti from the Wile E. Coyote cartoons that stand on ridge lines with their arms up, like they're waving hello or reaching for the sky during a stick-up. The road opens up and gives me a big shoulder. Walking is effortless.

In the morning while packing I hear a ripping sound. A quick check of the pants reveals nothing. At night I feel a draft, and sure enough there's a six-inch tear in my shorts, one that's been there all day as I strolled past the shops, restaurants, and yes, the school yards of Superior. Good thing I didn't go commando.

Camp off a side road on a perfectly flat alluvial plain. Dream beneath a desert sky. At dawn the lights of the huge city glow to the north like a fire just below the horizon. Billboards appear, then new traffic signals where housing developments are being built. Old people hit golf balls across a course of sand and pebbles. A flattened coyote, covered in tar, eyes closed and mouth open like it's screaming, lies on the shoulder where road crews were working. Traffic. Strip malls. Phoenix.

A big city, 60 miles across. I've written off three whole days to get across it.

Dirt in my eyes as I walk in and the wind picks up, hard. A dust storm erases the sky to the south, a boiling wall a thousand feet high that rolls in like the end of days. More dirt in my nose, grinding between my teeth, mixed with sweat and pasted to my forehead. The sky is orange.

East Mesa is not the most family-friendly place, at least the part I see from the street — pawn shops, back-yard auto repair and a handful of strip joints, or "gentlemen's clubs," as the sign above the Desert Flame announces. In the same way that there's no such thing as used cars anymore — they're now "certified, pre-owned" — and Kentucky Fried Chicken magically became "KFC" when everyone figured out that fried foods will eventually kill you, strip joints have become "gentlemen's clubs." Is that fooling anyone?

"Honey, can you watch the kids tonight? The guys are meeting at the gentlemen's club to sip some port and discuss the implications of socio-economic change currently sweeping across the former Soviet republics of Central Asia."

"You boys have a good time."

I walk into a Subway restaurant to use the bathroom, and when I come out the lady behind the counter yells, "Restroom for customers only!" I pass a billboard with a smiling, grandmotherly old woman beaming down at me, like an Orwellian telescreen, chin resting on her hands with an eager, helpful look on her face ("I like you and I care about you. Buy my product."). Dumb frat boys drive up in a car and yell something at me through the window, no idea what they said but it wasn't friendly.

Bring back my small towns and empty spaces.

In Phoenix proper, or rather one of the suburbs closer to the heart of Phoenix — there are so many I can't keep track — Maxwell, another friend of a friend, picks me up and takes me back to his place for a couple of nights. I really want to call him Max, because it has fewer syllables and I'm feeling lazy, but he seems to like Maxwell so I suck it up and go with it. We stop at his friend Patrick's house — can't I just call him Pat? — who does bong rips for a full hour while engaging in polite chit-chat and coughing up bits of lung. They say "kick-ass" a lot, usually as an adjective, as when Patrick asks Maxwell what he knows about a certain canyon they've been wanting to raft through:

"I heard it's kick-ass."

Or it's used as a stand-alone affirmation, a way of saying "okay!" or "all right!," as when Patrick asks Maxwell if he and his dogs would like to join him in a trip down said canyon:

"Kick-ass!"

At home I meet Maxwell's three dogs — Taylor, Boomer and Petunia. Three distinct personalities. Actually, maybe only two. Labs Taylor and Boomer might be of the same brain, big, lovable goofballs that live to chase tennis balls in the backyard and eat each other's poop off the grass. Petunia is the elder matriarch who sometimes sits idly by, sometimes jumps in to regulate when the kids get out of hand or one of them steals her favorite napping spot.

I do nothing for a couple of days, then get restless. Don't know how to stop moving anymore. A rolling stone. Maxwell is kind enough to drop me where he picked me up so that I don't have to miss any miles. He tells a last story to entertain me, a worst-case scenario about a lunch break, being in a car and not being able to find a bathroom in time. Top guy, that Maxwell. I'll miss him.

I walk all day through the city. Say hello to a kid walking by with a skateboard under his arm.

"Hi."

"My mom says not to talk to strangers."

"Good advice."

I keep on. A lot of deaf people in this city. I lose count of how many look me in the eye and walk by silently when I say hello. I see a droopy-faced man in dirty jeans and a baseball cap coming my way, staring at the ground and looking angry. I've made it a point to greet everyone I meet — goes with the territory for a roaming goodwill ambassador such as myself — so as he approaches I smile and say hello.

"Don't talk to me."

His answer catches me off guard, so I do what comes naturally — I laugh in his face. Less confrontational than my redneck response back in Missouri, but still fraught with peril, as there's no snarling Boo-Boo to bail me out this time. And this guy's not your garden variety, country bumpkin alcoholic. He spins around, eyes bloodshot and bulging. He's high on something, sky high. His face is scratched and bloody, and there's snot streaming from his nose. He balls up his fists as I subconsciously edge behind BJ because, like I already said, better her than me, and this guy obviously has no idea what sort of baby jogger he's messing with. But before it gets ugly he thinks twice about it, mutters something incoherent and stalks off.

Billboards in the countryside are a travesty, like graffiti in a cathedral, but in the cities they're one of the few things that keep me entertained — that and starting fights by saying hello to meth addicts. In Phoenix I see billboards that say "I'm a Mormon," featuring wholesome-looking white people paired with happy minorities, I guess to dispel the notion that all Mormons are white and live in Utah. "55-and-over" gated communities compete for space with RV resorts and rows of RV dealerships. I pass the largest motor home I've ever seen, parked in a lot with orange banners and small American flags arranged around it. It's called the "Patriot Thunder." Only in America could such an audacious and wasteful thing somehow be associated with patriotism and love of country. The sticker on the window says that this used — sorry, I mean "certified, pre-owned" — brontosaurus has a manufacturer's suggested retail price of over half a million dollars, but that it can now be yours for the unbelievably low price of $349, 951.00. And it gets about five to seven miles to the gallon. That wasn't on the sticker. I had to look it up later. I tried asking the bored salesman trolling the sidewalk out front, but he sniffed and looked at us sideways, apparently surmising from our appearance that BJ and I could not afford, nor would we truly be interested in, a Patriot Thunder of our very own.

"Why do you want to know?" he asked.

"So I can make fun of it later in my book."

He laughed in my face and walked away. So that's what it feels like.

I've been lucky in Phoenix. I know a few people. This night I get picked up by Bobby, an old friend from an old job. We drive back to his house at the end of a winding street in one of those sprawling, sand-colored subdivisions Phoenix is known for. The building boom never stopped here, even after the housing bubble burst and the construction industry collapsed everywhere else. Phoenix just keeps expanding, despite it being one of those cities that really has no business existing in the middle of a desert. Like Las Vegas. Or Los Angeles. Or any other city in the Southwest.

Bobby and his wife, Nicole ("Just call her 'Babe'") own a home on the outer edge of their development, with open desert stretching away behind their backyard. A tiny, freshly dug grave lies beside the fence on the edge of their property. Ryder, their six-year-old son, shot a hummingbird out of the sky in mid-flight with his pellet gun. Bobby is unabashedly proud of that, while Nicole feigns shock and horror, because it's probably the appropriate response from a parent and it's obvious Dad isn't going to set the example. But she's secretly impressed. "That was bad-ass," she whispers, and I have to agree.

I spend a couple days at their house, not doing much. Impress the kids with my formidable cereal-eating skills. Make a care package for myself out of the best Halloween candy — the chocolate — but am forced to put some back after Ryder makes sad puppy face, a tactic I've used many times myself with great success. I do my best seal imitation, basking motionless on the couch for hours on end, watching cloud shadows drift across the flank of Superstition Mountain directly out back.

While on his deathbed in 1891, a German prospector was said to have revealed the location of a gold mine hidden among the cliffs and chasms of Superstition Mountain. He had stumbled upon it many years earlier after its original owners had been massacred by Apaches. The woman to whom he had revealed his secret, Julia Thomas, promptly began a search that would last the rest of her life. Financially broken from her efforts, her final years were spent selling maps, full of misinformation, that purported to show locations for the mine. Since then many a fool has died or disappeared hunting for the treasure of the Lost Dutchman Mine.

Bobby and I embark on a less ambitious expedition up the mountain. It's on a signposted trail shared by a dozen or so child-toting suburbanites out for an easy, hour-long hike. We walk beneath a ridge of rock spires that disappear into mist every few minutes. Over one last hump is a cleft with standing water at the bottom and a naturally varnished rock face rising above it. There are hundreds of petroglyphs carved into the dark stone, along with modern graffiti, etchings of tourists' names and scars from gunshots.

"Who does something like that?" Bobby asks in disgust, wondering how someone could ruin such a beautiful, ancient and irreplaceable thing. I've asked that same question many times in front of other ancient art panels that had been spray-painted, shot at, smashed with rocks, scratched over or rubbed off. What kind of person looks at this artwork — which has outlived its maker by a thousand years, sitting in supreme isolation beneath the stars and the wind and the shadows of clouds — then makes the conscious decision to destroy it in a matter of seconds?

One of the most famous rock paintings in North America sits in a red rock canyon a few hundred miles from here. It's not particularly large, only a few feet across, and it's not particularly old as rock art goes, maybe 700 years. What makes it famous is its coloring and design — a round figure painted in red, white, and blue, which appears to have something resembling an American flag on its body. Hippies and new age mystics have gotten a bit carried away with it, believing it proof that ancient indigenous people foresaw the coming of white men and the founding of the United States. I had seen this painting several times in books and magazines, but no one ever said where it was. Many years later I stumbled upon it by accident in a remote sandstone canyon, its presence betrayed by handholds carved into a cliff face. Only a dozen feet above the ground was a shallow alcove. I scrambled up to find a partially ruined mud-and-rock wall jutting from the side of the cave. And there, right beside it, exactly as I remembered it, was the painting I had seen all those years ago in pictures.

I was struck by how close to the mouth of the cave it sat, so old but so vulnerable, looking as if it might disappear the next time the wind blew rain into the lip of the cave. It gave me goose bumps. I've felt the same way wandering through ancient temples, castles and cathedrals, or standing in front of a Rembrandt or a Monet. This was every bit as powerful, maybe more so due to the feeling of discovery and the remoteness of the cave. I sat in front of it, two feet away. No glass between us, no sign telling me what not to do, no guards. And that's why no one ever revealed where it was. Its remoteness and the fact that it's not marked on a map with a giant red "X" have saved it. To destroy it would be a crime against humanity. I hope that painting sits there forever. I hope it never suffers the fate of those at Superstition Mountain.

I leave Bobby and his family and continue my crawl through Phoenix. Still meeting people with hearing issues, people who just stare at me in silence. Unless I get menaced or propositioned there's little on my walk to distract me. I keep my head down and trudge through the last of the suburbs.

The city finally, mercifully ends at the White Tank Mountains. Sidewalks and shopping malls give way to dirt trails and sand hills within a span of five minutes. Pace slows, spirit rises. The interstate recedes behind me. Phoenix is a white line between the shell of the sky, and of the earth, and then it is nothing.

The desert. It feels like home. For the first time in two-thousand miles the fences come to an end. But access comes with a price. It's become a dump. Mattresses, sofas, TVs, computers, animal carcasses, microwave ovens, kitchen sinks, ruined cars. Spent ammunition casings glitter in the sun. Shattered glass crunches under my feet. Plastic bags cling to cacti like parasites.

It's hard to be an optimist today. Hard to have faith. Hard to see the human race as more than a global extinction event, the second coming of the meteor that wiped out the dinosaurs. On days like this I look at us and all I see are a few shining lights and a whole lot of cattle.

I'm being cynical again. It's one of the things I wanted to purge on this journey, as if six months of walking would wring out the darkness and leave something resembling wisdom in its place. Foolishness. I still want to apply labels, I still want people to fit neatly into the categories I've carved out for them. I want things to be black and white, not grey. But every day I meet people whose ideas about the world I just can't fathom, yet they surprise me with their kindness. Some are admitted criminals, some are racists, some are religious nuts and some hold political views that would have us killing each other if we dared discuss them. And some of them almost certainly throw shit on the ground in the middle of the desert. Yet they show me grace, and they show me love. Good to keep that in mind, I guess. Spirit engaged, mind in the right place. One foot in front of the other.

Gunfire is coming from several directions. I can't tell what's real and what's an echo. I walk a bit farther and set up camp in a shallow wash behind a cluster of creosote bushes. More rounds go off a hundred yards away. I peek around the bushes to see three guys quick-drawing on an old computer screen, like gunslingers facing off in the Old West. Only the computer screen doesn't shoot back (unfortunately), so it's more of an assassination. They blast it once, twice, three times, then once more for good measure. It wobbles a bit but won't go down. So they walk right up and unload on it from about three feet, firing away execution-style like mobsters settling a bad debt. It's a miracle no one has blown off a foot or a kneecap. The computer screen flops dramatically on its back. They stop to reload. This looks bad. I figure I'd better let them know I'm here before they mistake me for an animal, a hippie, or worse yet, a walking computer screen.

I call out from a long way off. The shooting stops. I make it to the clearing and see the three of them leaning against a giant Hot Wheels truck, lifted so high off the ground it has small ladders bolted to the sides so they can climb into the cab. They're in dirty wife-beaters and trucker hats worn backwards. Beer bottles litter the ground. I'm becoming cynical again.

I ask them what they're shooting at.

"Anything. We like to tear shit up."

They return to their work, blasting random pieces of junk scattered around the desert. An old clock. A tea kettle. A washing machine takes two to the chest. They find a recently discarded pumpkin and try to shoot a smiley face into it. When that doesn't work they send it to hell with a shotgun. Then one of them — they all look the same to me — throws a beer bottle and tries to shoot it out of the air. Time to leave. At midnight more gunfire, a lot of it, from the other side of the hill. No idea what they're shooting at in the middle of the night. It goes on for a couple of hours. At 2 a.m. I get up and walk.

The moon is a smudge behind a veil of cloud, a light left on behind a curtain. At this end, the Tonopah-Salome Highway is little more than a scratch on the desert floor. I don't know why they call it a highway. Sixty years ago maybe. Now it's a backwater of dirt and gravel, with a car every couple of hours during the day. At this hour there's nothing. The coyotes are out again, they never leave, even with World War III raging in the hills around them. I keep walking. The blasts grow fainter. Soon the only sounds are the crunch of gravel under BJ's tires and the din of the interstate three miles away, a gentle rumble like distant water. Every mile or so a lonely cabin, dimly lit by a sputtering overhead light, glows like a satellite in deep space. The night is windless and cold. The desert shimmers. From the corners of my eyes I see dark figures standing silent and motionless, watching me as I pass. Saguaros. Unseen creatures rustle in the creosote. I turn off my headlamp and walk into the darkness.

Tonopah looks like a Martian outpost. A gas station, a fast food joint, a diner and a hot spring on the south side of I-10, a last-chance bathroom break between Phoenix and Blythe.

My lonely road runs west. It can't decide if it wants to be a mess of shattered pavement or a washboard hell of gravel and sand, so it settles on a little of both. People told me this stretch would be boring, but I knew better. I've never seen an ugly desert. This far out the trash has disappeared. No more broken recliners and box springs. I walk across a plain of minor hills and scattered rocks, too insignificant to have names, mountain remnants melting away like the spine of a dinosaur sinking back into the earth. Weather is moving through in waves of rain and cloud and red dying sunlight. Sixty miles away the Castle Dome Mountains rise from the clouds like islands in a foamy sea.

Climb a hill, throw my pack against a rock, lay my head down on it. Yesterday I didn't believe in God. Today I do. Today I want to live to be a thousand years old. Not because I'm afraid of dying. Because I want to experience it all. I want to see everything there is to see. And I want every day to end like this one.

I need this like I need air in my lungs.

The road bends around a wash choked with scrub and low desert trees. More gunfire. A short time later a kid appears out of the brush with a shotgun and a bandolier of red shells across his chest. His name is George. He's a quail hunter. Has a couple dead birds in a plastic grocery bag around his waist. Nice kid. At 13 I trust him more with a gun than virtually any of the adults I've met out here. We talk for a few minutes and he explains the finer points of quail hunting.

"You walk through the trees. Then, when you see 'em, you blast 'em."

He says his dad has an assault rifle that can shoot three miles.

I ask him how he got out here.

"Drove."

He says he likes BJ and he's not joking. I think that's the first time anyone's said that with a straight face. He walks back into the bushes and disappears.

I've met a few people who say they've died and come back. The religious ones see lights and angels and maybe God himself. A man in Missouri told me he heard popcorn going off in his head after nearly drinking himself to death and going into a coma. A woman in New Hampshire told me she died on the operating table and had an out-of-body experience, the kind you see acted out and described in chilling fashion by Leonard Nimoy on old television programs. Is it real? Or is it just a manifestation of a frightened mind in its final, dying moments?

At times I've wished I'd had a near-death experience. Nothing that actually hurt or did damage. Something quick and painless. Like being on an airliner that loses power and plunges 20,000 feet, enough time for my life to flash before my eyes and show me all the things I'd never done but wished I had, all my regrets, before pulling out of it at the last second, the pilot then getting on the horn and saying something understated and soothing like, "Sorry for the bumpy ride, folks, should be clear sailing from here to Chicago . . ."

Something to wake me up. To make me stop wasting time. A reminder to live every day.

Today I meet Tim, cycling across America. Tim had a near-death experience, a car crash in the snow with a big rig sliding sideways down an icy highway straight into him. But his wasn't easy and painless; maybe these things can't be. He spent a long time in the hospital, and came out a changed man.

He forgave the woman he divorced eight years ago and fell in love with someone else. He let go of anger, resentment, everything. He holds on to nothing, whatever he thinks or feels just flows right through him and out his mouth, for better or worse, usually for better.

What happened to you?

"I found freedom."

What more is there?

"Wisdom."

Tim, 57 years old, searching for wisdom on the highways of America. We say goodbye and head in opposite directions, several orders of separation between us.

I think I'm going feral. I still brush my teeth and change my underwear most days, but I've become comfortable with smelling like a horse's butt. The possibility of a shower comes up and I'll say to myself, "Nah, I just had one three days ago." I've taken to howling out loud for no good reason, hoping the coyotes will answer back, and sometimes they do. I sing all the time, sleep outside curled up on the ground, partly because the zippers on my tent have completely failed and partly because I just don't care anymore. I get up at midnight and walk through the desert. I hear animals all around me, mostly small ones. I sit and listen for hours.

The mascot at Salome High School is an angry frog. I stop to contemplate that for a moment, wondering why someone couldn't have made half an effort to come up with something better. A man drives up and tells me that this one school serves 3,400 square miles, and that kids come from 90 miles away to attend. I tell him that if I had to drive 180 miles round-trip to go to school, I'd just choose illiteracy.

"That's why you're pushin' a baby stroller down the highway."

I stop at a diner and a kid is throwing a fit three booths over. Haggard, exhausted mother is trying to feed the baby, inattentive father is talking sports on a cell phone. Kid starts knocking dishes off the table, neither parent reacts. Screaming, banging on the table. Old ladies at the next table are horrified but too nice to say anything. I'm not too nice, but I'm also three booths over and highly entertained. Now the kid is up on the bench marching like a storm trooper. Now he's on the table itself. Parents still checked out, dad on the cell phone.

And just as I'm swearing off kids forever, a little girl leans over from the next booth as I'm stuffing an omelet and a triple stack of pancakes down my throat.

"You eat a lot."

"That's an astute observation."

"What's 'astoot?'"

I start explaining but her mother snaps at her to turn around and stop bothering the nice but crazy man. The conversation comes to an abrupt end, but not before she smiles again at me, restoring my faith in adorable children everywhere.

Back in Maine I started taking pictures of the many badly worded signs I came across. I had an idea to assemble them into a slideshow for my maybe girlfriend, who as an English major and journalist is horrified by public displays of bad grammar and poor punctuation. On the far side of Hope I find a good one, maybe the concluding slide of my show, strong enough to draws oohs and ahhs from the snooty, college-educated intellectuals in attendance. It simply says "Your Beyond Hope," which I guess is a clever way to remind motorists that they've just sped through town and they had better turn around for a beer or a slice of pie before it's too late. And it would have been clever had they known how to use a contraction. But they didn't. And now their beautifully painted, hopelessly flawed tourist sign has become the prize of my snooty slideshow.

Another sign coming into Bouse — this one spelled correctly — says, "Home to 875 friendly people and 35 grouches." In a no-name bar there's a slat-wood painting of a naked Indian princess, certain parts covered by a blanket, certain parts not. It's the kind of thing you'd find at a garage sale for ten dollars, talk the guy down to eight, then proudly take it home and hang it in a moldy corner of the basement to gather dust forever after. There's a look on her face, a mystery in her smile.

A naked, flea-market Mona Lisa. I covet that painting. I desire it. I ask the bartender how much.

"A million dollars."

"I've got ten."

"Have another beer."

A big guy keeps coming up to the bar complaining that his beer "has a hole in it" and he wants another one. His shirt says, "Warning: This Vietnam Vet Heavily Medicated." His name is Richard. We only speak for a couple of minutes but I feel like there's a story in him that wants to get out. There are a lot of people in these places trying to escape from things — crowded cities, cold weather, child-support payments — and I want to know what Richard is running from. But I'm trying to make miles so I pass on it, and a mile down the road I wish I hadn't. What did he have to share with me?

The road is littered with beer bottles. Traffic gets worse and there are no shoulders. Drivers are becoming careless and rude. There's something in the air, something familiar. I come over a small hill and there it is: California, six miles away.

I make it to Parker and all I want to do is pass on through. Maybe because I'm looking forward to my final state, and to home, or because I already know what Parker is: snow-bird haven during the winter, throwaway party destination during spring break and summer. Signs saying "Welcome Winter Visitors" — a euphemism for "old people " — guide me into town. In the summer, when they shoo the oldies away and bar the gates to anyone under 30, those signs are replaced with ones that say "Welcome Drunken Community College

Students." Strange dichotomy. I can't imagine the two sides co-existing. What happens to the old people? Pack up the Patriot Thunders and head back to Wisconsin? Or do they ever leave? I pass a senior center and imagine old people shuffling in on one side and Soylent Green being loaded into trucks on the other. Calm down, man, you've been on the road too long. But I won't be eating any hot dogs in this town.

I don't pass through; a crummy motel is in order because BJ has an injury, and we need a place to relax and make a diagnosis. Our accommodation choices are: mediocre, bad, and really bad. One-star establishments charging three-star rates. A broken husk of a motel, a third-tier Vegas rip-off from the Frank Sinatra era, goes for $65 a night. Back in Tucumcari it would have been $19.95, and it would have been nicer.

I pass several of these rotting dilapidations before settling on the Budget Inn. I have a look at BJ and find a split tire, with a bare inner tube bulging out of a hole the size of a marble. It's a hernia, essentially. As before, the tire refuses to cooperate. Same problem — the tire fits so tightly on the rim I can't force it off. I wedge one, then two, then four tire irons between the rim and the lip of the tire. Lubricate the edge with shampoo to slip it off. Won't budge. I end up snapping all my plastic irons and hopelessly bending all the metal ones. I throw them against the wall and look at BJ in disgust. She sits in front of the T.V. in silence.

The honeymoon is over. Our flame flutters like a candle dying in a breeze. When we first started, every day was magical. There was a bounce in our step, a twinkle in our eyes. Every minute an adventure to be shared, together. Now she barely speaks, and when she does all I hear is complaining. And frankly, she's let herself go. Handlebar's scuffed and worn, rims don't shine like they used to and her seat is sagging a lot more than when we first met.

I find myself eyeing newer joggers in parks and town squares, pretty little things with their parts in all the right places, rolling along effortlessly with nary a rattle or squeak. But then she catches me looking and I never hear the end of it. I'm done with this — I want out. I'm ready to roll her off a bluff over the river to see how well she can fly, then find out if she can swim.

But then I remember all we've been through — the laughter, the crying, the good times and the bad. The unbreakable bond that forms between man and inanimate object. I settle down. We make up.

In the end, Walmart comes to the rescue. You can't incorporate a town in America anymore unless it has a Walmart. Anything less is no longer a town — it's a dump of leaning hovels and shoeless, bread-nibbling peasants. I repeal my standing boycott of said super store (don't ask, you don't want to know) because I have little choice, and, frankly, principle goes right out the window when I'm tired and cranky. The Evil Empire comes through with almost exactly what I need, or a cheaper and slightly substandard version of it. At this point the tire is history; a pair of wire cutters snips it off, biting through the metal bead on the rim that had, until now, been eating my tire irons and destroying my life.

Morning at the Early Bird Cafe, where the bartender and six crusty locals are engaging in light, racist banter about American Indians.

"Just give 'em alcohol . . ."

The T.V. news is on, and every time President Obama is mentioned slurs erupt from the gallery. It's all in good fun — like-minded, racist rednecks bonding over ignorance and a shared hatred of anyone not like themselves. I'm reminded again how different this walk would be if my skin were a different color. Or if I were overtly gay, or an outed liberal. As I leave the bartender says, "Come back sometime." I laugh and walk out the door, without tipping.

CALIFORNIA

Across the Colorado River, my last major water crossing. It's turquoise green and translucent, a tropical lagoon, a desert mirage. Large fish are holding position against the current with lazy strokes of their tails. It's not particularly wide, and will get narrower still after a couple more lakes and dams downstream, until it disappears altogether into the sands of Mexico. The mighty Colorado, architect of the Grand Canyon, lifeblood of the Southwest, no longer even joins with the sea, its massive volume sucked dry by cities, suburban lawns and agriculture before it ever gets there.

I want to linger but I can't, as they're doing construction on the bridge and I have to run across with traffic. On the other side, Dolores the construction worker scolds me like a concerned, exasperated grandmother — there's always one of these around when I do something stupid — then gives me a 7-Up and a reflective safety vest so drivers can see me. As I walk through the construction zone, other workers eye me with envy.

"Where'd you get that vest?"

"Rolled some guy down the road and stole it from him."

Nobody laughs, so I tell them the truth and one guy gets angry, muttering about how they cost $45 and his is about 2 years old and falling off his shoulders.

"No one ever gave me one . . ." he says in a hurt voice.

I consider giving it to him because I feel sorry for him. But then I realize how much safer I am with it, and I like how official it makes me look, like BJ and I are doing some sort of important work surveying the road instead of wandering aimlessly down it like we are.

It fools everyone else, too. Now people stop to ask me directions, thinking I'm someone who can tell them where they are. At some point in the near future a car will pull over and a nice lady in heels will get out and walk her happy, sniffing Dachshund up to me. "My husband is lost," she will say. "Can you help him get to Parker?" she will ask.

"Turn around and go 90 miles that way," I will tell them, pointing in the direction they just came from, because they drove right past it 90 miles ago.

"But my GPS said to turn right," he will say . . .

The Mojave Desert is vast and cruel, a place you drive across on the way to somewhere else while thinking, "Can you imagine *walking* across that?" I remind myself I'm still on a highway, so as long as my thumbs don't get nibbled off by rabid chipmunks I should be able to hitch a ride in an emergency. From the Arizona border it's 17 miles to Vidal Junction, which may or may not have a convenience store, no one seems to be sure, then 92 miles farther to Twentynine Palms with nothing in between. That's four days of walking.

But I don't mind. I love these huge expanses, these hundred-mile walks between towns. I love the freedom of it, the silence, the isolation. I love the loneliness.

The road parallels a railway for several hours, and on its sloping bed thousands of people have spelled out their names with rocks. I find a couple that say "BJ," but "Kent" is nowhere to be found. Mom and Jesus are well represented. There even seems to be a section for L.A. gangsters on holiday —

"Shooter," "Flaco," "Creepy" and "Puppet." A few stoners have spelled out "4:20." College students by the dozens have stopped to mark out fraternities and sororities on their way to Parker for a weekend of alcohol poisoning and careless sex. Someone even took the time to spell "boobies."

At night I see an unidentified flying object. Really. No idea what it is, only that it's unidentified, and that it's flying. Now, almost anything could be a U.F.O. — you could chuck a Frisbee off a building, and until someone identifies it as a Frisbee, it's a U.F.O. This one, which I see several times, looks like a flare that dies out and reignites at intervals, seven or eight times in a line across the sky. Too high to be fireworks. Too erratic to be a plane. I never do see any little green men, and to my knowledge I was never abducted or probed in any way, though I hear they're pretty good at wiping memories. Probably just a flare.

Fighter jets roar down the valley every hour, always the same, along the line of hills, hard bank to the left, followed by a steep, spinning climb, then disappearing over the next mountain range. I see small, tattered American flags planted in the sand next to mile markers. Beside one is a placard that says "Race For the Fallen," with a picture of a U.S. soldier on it. U.S. Army Sgt. Timothy Hayslett, killed in Iraq by a grenade, leaves a wife and two young daughters. Don't know if it was forgotten or left there on purpose, but it somehow seems right, fluttering in the breeze like a prayer flag, sending his name down the valley and off to heaven every time the wind blows.

A desert sunset. A mix of wind-blown dust, Los Angeles smog and God just showing off. A masterpiece, with every gradation of color from hot pink to muted grey as the sun sinks at one end of the valley and night creeps in at the other. We quicken our pace, trying to make it last a little longer. Stars appear in the half light, shimmering above granite boulders that sit in dumb silence in the emptiness of the desert. A distant mountain catches the last light of the day. Sky fades to purple. Sky fades to black.

Even here I'm still meeting people. I stop to take a picture of a giant red rooster, made of plaster, sitting atop an abandoned building. A man walks up to do the same. He tells me he lived in Hawaii for 40 years and that he hates the ocean. Hates the ocean? Is that possible? An obscene statement, akin to Hannibal Lecter announcing he's going to eat a man's liver with some fava beans and a nice Chianti. I dislike him instantly but don't know what to say. We stare at the rooster for an awkward moment, then retreat in opposite directions.

I meet another person, this one much more rational. Salva from Spain. He's been riding his bike around the world for the past five years. From Europe to Africa, all the way around the edges, the Middle East, the coasts of India, island hopping across Indonesia, into China and Japan, to Alaska, through Canada and now here, nowhere, the middle of the desert. He expects to be on the road four more years. Where to next? "Argentina." Thinks Americans are overwhelmingly friendly but afraid of the world, with little understanding of places outside the U.S.A.

In the ghost town of Rice people have been hanging shoes, bras and underwear on a tree and a nearby fence for decades. There are literally thousands of them. I inspect a few bras — they just seem more interesting than shoes — when I notice a minivan parked a short distance away. I immediately switch to shoe inspection but don't think I'm fooling anyone. A young family from Australia piles out, a couple and two small children. They've traveled through South America for four months, now five more months in a van across America. The man is some sort of computer genius who gets paid to work out of a minivan while traveling the world. They tell me of sights on the Altiplano of Bolivia that every person should see before they die. They give me a Pacifico for the road. And they don't say anything about the bras.

In Kansas and across the Panhandle I was constantly misjudging distances. In the morning I'd see a grain silo on the horizon and figure I'd be there in two hours, but I wouldn't reach it till sundown. So it is in the desert. At night I camp on a low saddle between two mountains and see the lights of cars creeping across the alluvial plain I crossed at dawn, hurtling through the darkness like rockets. But at 85 miles an hour it still takes them 20 minutes to reach me.

My tent sits in a wash below a great jumble of shattered boulders, like the broken ramparts of a ruined castle. Highway 62 is the northern boundary of Joshua Tree National Park, and the pink granite that makes the park famous doesn't stop at the highway. Giant marbles have rolled north across the road to the slanting gravel plain on the other side, coming to rest at the edges of dry lakes and sand dunes. I hide behind them to shelter from the wind and blowing sand. The ground is often littered with tarnished bullet casings, blackened with age and clogged with mud and clay, providing housing for spiders and beetles that crawl out whenever I pick one up.

I sit on a rock with my Pacifico and a can of Spaghettios. I watch the desert, admiring the simplicity of it, the uncluttered perfection. Everything in its right place. A scratching noise to my right catches my attention. A haggard creosote bush is tracing perfect circles in the dirt around its base with hanging limbs, etching the ground whenever the wind picks up, a natural compass of breeze and twig.

The creosote is an underappreciated plant. From a distance it looks like a giant weed, the sort of nondescript bush travelers might stop to take a leak on or hang their socks from while sitting around the campsite. It gets little respect. But it's one of the toughest plants you'll ever find. Its roots absorb water so efficiently they dry out the soil around them, making it impossible for seeds of competing plants to germinate. Indians used it to cure diarrhea, alleviate kidney pain and soothe wounds. And they live forever, or close to it: a group of them in California's Lucerne Valley is thought to be nearly 12,000 years old.

I hang my socks and underwear from the creosote — sorry, it's just so handy — and have a look around. The sand around my tent is covered with the braided tracks of animals —

insects, scorpions, birds, snakes, coyotes, tarantulas, centipedes and kangaroo rats. The rats I see everywhere, and they do look like tiny kangaroos, with tails longer than their bodies and the ability to jump up to nine feet despite standing only a few inches tall. I find their little bodies all over the side of the highway, for some reason seldom smashed, looking like they're just taking an afternoon siesta.

One thing I don't find is a desert tortoise, though I spend a few hours looking. They hold a special place in my heart because my brother and I once owned one as little kids. Our tortoise was named "Go-Go," because he really went-went, and he did it really fast. At least for a tortoise. My dad built him his own little house, with a slanted tile roof and an oval entryway so he could sit inside and do exciting things like watch the grass grow or sleep all day. At the end of autumn he'd disappear into his house and not come back out, so we'd pack it with crumpled newspapers and move it into a corner of the tool shed, where Go-Go would sleep all winter.

In the spring he'd be ready to go, sometimes too ready, as when he'd come out early before my dad had a chance to move him back out and we'd find Go-Go doing feverish laps around the lawnmower. A big head of iceberg lettuce would then be devoured, followed by some unauthorized roaming if we turned away for about 20 seconds. This is how he earned his name — he'd take off and go-go. We'd search for him, following his little tracks in circles around the bottlebrush and winding around the back of the hibiscus. He'd usually head straight for the cactus garden on the side of the house, which he bull-dozed and ate on several occasions. If we didn't find him there, we'd call out Rusty, our faithful German shepherd.

"Rusty! Where's Go-Go? Where's Go-Go at? Where is he? Go find him, boy! Go get him!"

And Rusty would get really excited and run off, sniffing around the bottlebrush and behind the hibiscus. He'd always find our little tortoise. But if we didn't get to Go-Go quickly, Rusty would flip him onto his back and shovel him across the grass with his nose like a hockey puck.

I spent long minutes on my stomach watching him, looking at his little old man face and wondering what wisdom he tucked away in there that he never revealed to us. Then we grew up and no one paid attention to him anymore, which is probably just the way he liked it. My dad found a crazy lady who had converted her backyard into some sort of turtle/tortoise sanctuary, like a Disneyland for crawling reptiles. And there Go-Go went. He was about 50 years old at the time and I'm sure he's still around, watching the grass grow.

I tire of hunting wild Go-Gos and return to camp. I sleep outside; I stare at the sky. The moon is out. The boulders glow. I hear small noises between sighs of the wind. BJ begins to growl. A miniature avalanche of pebbles and sand falls from the top of the rock pile. What was that? I regret not setting up my tent, my little diving bell, whose nylon walls have protected me from ticks, zombies, ghosts and serial killers since the haunted forests of New England. I dive into my sleeping bag and zip it over my head.

My isolation comes to an end outside Twentynine Palms. To the north, the lights and scattered outliers of the Marine Corps Air Ground Combat Center, the largest U.S. Marine Corps base in the world, glow in the early morning. The desert becomes a checkerboard of development and degraded open space where people have dumped old sofas and driven off-road vehicles in every direction. Broken-down homesteads appear. Most seem to be abandoned or otherwise uninhabited, but chained outside several of them are dogs that start barking a quarter-mile before I pass and keep going for the same distance afterward.

On the edge of town I get rushed by three of these huge dogs — unchained this time — a Rottweiler and two pit bulls, who look fearsome but are really just giant mush balls looking for a treat. They run clear across the highway, oblivious to traffic, but luckily there isn't any. One goes straight for the trash bag under BJ, like a lion on the Serengeti eviscerating a hapless gazelle, flinging innards of garbage all over the place. Two of the dogs then lie down in the middle of the highway eating Snickers wrappers covered in ants, courtesy of the mobile ant farm that's been living inside BJ for the past week. The third, a one-eyed bulldog, just watches, squinting at me as if weighing the benefits of chewing crusty, beer-soaked candy wrappers (sprinkled with ants) or lunging straight at my guts for some fresh menudo. The owner, also one-eyed (yes, people really do look like their pets) is wearing a filthy Dallas Cowboys jacket and a beret. He wanders over and introduces himself as Clark.

Clark is exactly the type of person you'd expect to find living on the margins of society, in a desert shack with no running water, garbage piled to the roof and three crazy dogs running around loose. Of course I like him. Clark is into conspiracy theories, and is convinced the government is trying to control us through sugar. He says when he was young, the government forced everyone to take three sugar cubes laced with a vaccine to inoculate against polio. He ate two of them, then realized what was really happening — that the government was secretly trying to take control of his mind — so he spat out the third one and ran away before the takeover could be completed. He found his way to the desert, where he's been a colossal pain in the ass to local officials and newspapers ever since.

He's fought every traffic ticket or parking citation he ever got. He's trying to sue a judge. He set up security cameras in his house and caught a woman walking through his living room stealing things (where were the dogs?). Now he's trying to figure out "how to handle the problem" because he doesn't trust the police. He drinks a lot of beer and smokes pot constantly in protest against excessive government meddling in our lives. I temp fate by asking him if I can take a photo, assuming he'll brand me a government agent and have the mush balls tear me limb from limb. But he just smiles and says okay.

A bit farther down the road I'm in Twentynine Palms proper, walking on a sidewalk in town when a car pulls up with a giant sofa on top, exactly the kind you might find illegally dumped in the desert. Two middle-aged guys stumble out, completely wasted. I ask them what they're doing with the sofa.

"Dumping it."

One is named Dwayne and the other mumbles so much I can't understand him. The left side of Dwayne's skull has a huge dent in it. I ask him what happened and he tells me a convoluted story about cheating on a girlfriend who then got angry and ran over his head with a '69 Chevy van. They're very high, jittery and twitching, and when they speak they're six inches from my face, sour beer breath and weed wafting from their mouths. They're really interested in my walk and start following me around, asking the same questions over and over because they keep forgetting that they already asked them.

"Where'd you walk from?"

"Maine."

"You really walking, man?"

"Yeah."

"Whoa. Where'd you walk from?"

"Maine."

They seem as surprised on the second or third time they hear the answers as they were on the first. At least they're enthusiastic.

"You ever done acid?" the mumbler mumbles.

"No."

"Want to?"

"No, but thanks for asking."

I ask if I can take their picture, which makes them happy. There's no chance of anything candid, because as soon as I raise the camera they start flashing gang signs. Then they start beating each other over the head with water weenies — those hollow foam tubes that kids play with in the pool and float on to keep from drowning — which are inexplicably piled up in the back seat. Sensing an opportunity for escape, I egg them on a bit, directing them by saying stupid things like, "That's a good one!", "Hit him again!", "In the face!" and "Harder!" They're really getting into it, screaming, sweating and turning pink from getting slapped in the face. Thus distracted, I'm able to bail around the corner, zig-zagging down a few streets to lose them. Later in the evening I see them across the street, sitting on the curb with a police cruiser pulled up alongside, lights flashing.

Twentynine Palms, Joshua Tree and Yucca Valley bleed together and make for uneventful walking. Lots of fast food, lots of garbage. A nice but crazy Mongolian lady at a bus stop gives me a strawberry dipped in chocolate on a stick, but the strawberry falls into the gutter before I can take a bite and I'm left licking a chocolaty stick.

The scenery beyond the towns is still beautiful. I can see why people live here, at least in the winter. Joshua trees, the namesake of the national park I've been walking beside, appear only at the highest crest of the road and then disappear just as quickly before the downhill beyond. The trees, which are often likened to the whimsical plants found in Dr. Seuss books, were named by Mormon settlers in the 19th century, who thought their craggy, upturned arms looked like the Biblical Joshua reaching his hands skyward to God.

The road becomes dangerous, a steep downhill with shoulders that go from six feet to one and back again, with the narrowest parts on the sharpest, blindest curves. Not quite the Highway of Death but it has its moments. Ironically, just before climbing out of the desert I come to the driest, most barren part of it — the low, sandy waste around Palm Springs that is, in the summer, one of the hottest spots in the nation. I pass between two dramatic peaks, San Gorgonio on the right and San Jacinto on the left, each over 10,000 feet and covered in snow.

Another surprise. My dad arrives. Not a surprise really, because he called me beforehand this time instead of just magically appearing like he did in New Mexico. And this time he only drove 60 miles instead of 600.

He treats me to a hotel in Palm Springs, home to celebrities, wealthy retirees and impossibly green golf courses springing from the dead sand courtesy of rapidly depleting underground aquifers. We relax, watch some T.V., then do some reconnaissance of the route ahead. One of the roads I want to walk on is barred by a gate and a man with a bullet-proof vest and a gun. This is the border of the Morongo Indian Reservation. We pull over just before the gate and the guard cautiously approaches. I step out to meet him and his hand moves to his hip, as if he thinks he might actually have to shoot me for approaching too closely.

"Can I help you?"

Which, of course, really means: "What the hell do you want?" Or maybe: "Please do something stupid so I can shoot you."

"I'm walking across America. I can't walk on the interstate, and I don't think there are any other roads I can walk on. Can I walk through here tomorrow?"

"No."

"Why not?"

"We're a sovereign nation."

I see. That of course answers nothing. Switzerland is a sovereign nation and you don't see them barricading the borders with gates and armed guards. I stand there for a moment trying to figure out why it's such a big deal. Is there an illegal immigration problem, with U.S. citizens fleeing the country clubs of Palm Springs to stream across the border and steal jobs from Morongo Indians? Too many Jehovah's Witnesses knocking on doors? Just want to keep out that troublesome non-Morongo element?

Maybe the problem is money. There's a huge casino here raking in hundreds of millions of dollars a year. The Morongo Band of Mission Indians distributes some of this money among its thousand or so members to the tune of $30,000 per adult per month. Apparently there's so much left over they don't know what to do with it. So they build gates and hire security guards. I personally have no problem with Indian casinos. It goes without saying that American Indians have been getting screwed for the last 500 years or so, and before this casino was built the reservation might not have been a pleasant place to live in. I also understand the idea of not letting just anyone prowl around your neighborhood — like you, I hate having to slam the door when adorable Girl Scouts come knocking, especially when they're selling Thin Mints, which I can barely resist. But I don't really get the purpose of turning your land into an exclusive club, walling yourselves off from the rest of America just because you can, or because you want to stick your tongue out at everyone else, fellow Indians of less-fortunate tribes included.

In the end, the guard doesn't shoot me, though he looks slightly disappointed. He turns out to be a pretty nice guy. Just doing his job, I know. He has me wait a bit longer while he lets a couple of acceptable vehicles pass through, each time pressing a button that lowers a thick metal barrier into the ground, which then rises immediately afterward, lest any *Dukes of Hazzard* types try to jump across before it closes. Then he takes a minute to show me an alternative route I didn't know existed.

My dad takes the jogger for the day so I can walk like a normal person and not have to endure "Hey Doris, there's that dumb guy with the baby stroller" stares. I pass through the giant wind turbines of the San Gorgonio Pass, marveling at their size. They're soothing to watch, like a herd of giraffes congregating on a hillside. Many of them are not working, with burnt holes at the head where the blades connect, as if they were struck by lightning or someone chucked a grenade at them.

This is the transition zone out of the desert, so I start the day surrounded by sand and cacti and end it in rolling hills of green grass. The highlight is passing the Cabazon dinosaurs — Dinny, a 45-foot tall concrete Apatosaurus, and Mr. Rex, an equally massive Tyrannosaurus Rex. Apparently, this classic piece of roadside Americana is now owned by creationists seeking a fun way to debunk evolution.

In the afternoon I see a kid walking the other way wearing a giant backpack with all sorts of junk dangling off the sides.

"Where are you going?" I ask him.

"Walking across America."

"What a coincidence . . . "

I've met a lot of people cycling across the country. I wonder how many do it each year. Hundreds for sure. Possibly thousands. I've met many other people who initially claim to have crossed the country on foot. After finding out what I'm doing, they will say something like this:

"Oh yeah, me and Bob did that 20 years ago. Jumped trains like hobos from Tuscaloosa to San Francisco. . ."

Or they'll say:

"Yep. Me and my cousin Jeb did that once. Hitchhiked from Oregon to South Carolina to watch my pappy march down the aisle for the fifth time . . ."

But I'm not jumping trains or hitchhiking. This kid is the first one I've met who is doing what I'm doing, walking across America. Jesse from Indiana — blond, skinny, excited, looks like he's going to fall over under that pack, just like I did. He's just starting, walking from California to Florida to raise money for a children's hospital where he spent some time after being burned in a fire. He's right on the edge of the desert, already complaining about the pack weight and not yet started the same hundred miles of nothing I just came through. "Better get a jogger," I say. He nods solemnly.

Walking across America. This guy must be crazy.

A momentous occasion. BJ has been retired. My friend, my muse, my little burro. My constant companion. When we began I was so self conscious I had to correct people when they called her a baby stroller — "It's a *jogger*," I would say, as if that sounded more acceptable — now she's so much a part of me I don't know what to do without her. I find myself lifting my hands for the handlebar that's no longer there, an amputee with a phantom limb. But I don't need her anymore. The huge empty spaces are past, places to eat and drink are plentiful and the final route I'm planning through the mountains is a nominal footpath through a treacherous canyon, impossible for her to traverse. So I take her apart, fold her in half and shove her in a corner of my parents' garden shed to sleep with the earwigs and spiders. She's earned her retirement.

But it will be short-lived. Some months down the line BJ will ride again. Only this time she'll be doing something a little more sensible, like carrying a good friend's pretty, blue-eyed little girl down neighborhood sidewalks instead of dodging semis and cow turds for 3,000 miles. Something a little more in line with what her creator had in mind.

I thought this walk would make me tough. It hasn't. I can't believe how hard it is to hike with the backpack again, even though it only weighs 35 pounds. Feet hurt, ankles hurt, knees ache. Just one more week to go.

South of Beaumont it gets pretty again, steep hills covered with giant granite boulders, followed by flat plains and dairy farms. I can tell I'm getting close to home when I see a billboard with two big eyeballs staring down from it that says, "Sex Offenders: We're Watching You!"

In a small, fenced field there are two little dogs, a miniature pony, a cow, a goat and a llama, all milling about in perfect harmony. They stare at me as I walk by, heads turning silently in unison. On my side of the road a bored sheep dog is making a half-hearted attempt at herding his flock, until he looks up and decides to herd me instead. He barks a few times, but very friendly, tail wagging, crisscrossing in front of me, barking some more, running in circles, completely ignoring the sheep he's supposed to be watching.

"Is herding sheep really that boring?" I ask.

He looks at me sideways and keeps jogging.

"Bark once for yes and twice for no."

He wags his tail.

"Well there's the problem. You don't speak English. Maybe you don't speak 'sheep' either."

He barks twice.

"So you're just lazy?"

A single bark.

"If you worked for me I'd fire you."

He sticks his tongue out. No, he's just panting.

I ask a few more questions but get the silent treatment, so I throw a piece of beef jerky at him and he runs away, happy.

It gets more developed and I think I might have a problem finding a campsite. But just in time a huge field appears around the bend, bisected by an irrigation canal lined with bushes and shrubbery. I set up beneath a tree. An owl is hooting on a branch above. I make the slightest movement and it swoops away, silently. Croaking frogs and rustling leaves drown out the traffic.

At dawn I hear crows. Lots of crows. I unzip the tent and look out to see hundreds of them — hundreds upon hundreds — sitting on the power lines by the road, in the tree over my head and standing in the field all around the tent. The noise stops when they see me. They turn to stare, all of them at once, with black, soulless eyes, like a herd of evil garden gnomes. A Hitchcock moment. I toss a pebble at the nearest group and they don't budge, because they recognize my limp throw for what it is — a lame, half-hearted bluff.

I decide right then, based on lazy conjecture and a sliver of evidence, that crows are extremely intelligent. If these were pigeons they wouldn't budge either, but that's because pigeons are stupid. They've been lulled into a false sense of security by long hours spent scrounging French fries from under restaurant tables and pilfering kibble from the backyard doggie dish. No one ever goes after them because they're not worth the trouble, and if you were to take one out, another would just pop up in its place like a cockroach. You could walk right up to one and stomp it to death before it knew what was happening, such is the laziness and stupidity of pigeons. You could never do that to a crow. Crows think. They analyze. They measure and perceive threats accurately. To prove my point I zing another pebble into the middle of them. Those in the line of fire deftly hop out of the way, floating gently back down once the pebble has passed. That throw would have knocked out the first pigeon and scattered the rest of the flock in panic, wasting valuable lounging time in the process. I decide to not throw any more pebbles because I realize how much I respect crows, and because they're starting to look really angry. I pack up quickly and get moving.

The backpack feels lighter today, just a matter of getting used to it again. Not much happens. Highlight of the day is a huge split boulder that someone has painted to look like a sliced watermelon. Camp on a gravel spit jutting into Lake Elsinore, watching herons and egrets fishing in the shallows, silhouetted against city lights reflecting off the water.

THE CANYON

The Santa Anas aren't much as mountains go, a minor range running 40 miles from end to end, topping out at 5,689-foot Santiago Peak. High enough to get snow a few times a year and low enough to have it melt after a day or so. In these mountains I'll have my final adventure.

I have two other options to the sea: follow the freeway for five days of urban sprawl and zero camping, or test my mortality on Ortega Highway, a twisting mountain road locally famous for car crashes, dead motorcyclists, and as a convenient dumping place for murder victims from Riverside and Orange counties. Helpful hint: if you come across a rolled up carpet or leaky trash bag off the side of this road, don't investigate.

From a walking standpoint, this would be the most dangerous highway of my entire journey, far worse than my Highway of Death back in Arizona. More traffic, sharper curves, no shoulders. Suicide with a jogger. People do crazy things on this road, like pass on double-yellow blind corners so dangerous I assumed they were trying to kill themselves, because if anyone were to be coming from the other direction — likely given the heavy traffic — there would be a head-on collision with multiple fatalities.

Third option is to find my own way across these mountains by way of back roads, game trails and bushwhacking. Mostly bushwhacking. I am aiming for a specific canyon, one I've been to many times by myself, and a few times with friends. Once with a girl I had a huge crush on (nothing happened).

Finding my way shouldn't be a problem. Once into the canyon, the walls are so high and steep there's almost no chance of getting lost as long as I stay at the bottom. Just follow it downstream to the end, where it conveniently pops out beside the highway after bypassing the most dangerous parts of the road. What could possibly go wrong?

There once were gray wolves here. Condors too, and even grizzly bears, which thrived in the lower elevations into the 1860s, when they were inevitably hunted out. The last bear was shot in 1908. Her hide is now in the Smithsonian Institution. Besides coyotes, the only big predators left are mountain lions, though in all my years hiking through the West and into Mexico, I have never seen one.

Rattlesnakes are always a danger, though at this time of year they're probably hibernating or too groggy to bother with a fat, juicy ankle placed alluringly in front of their lairs. In this same place I once encountered three large rattlers on the trail within a half an hour. The first one was easy to spot, lying in the middle of the trail like a coiled rope dropped by a hiker. The second one I heard but never saw, rattling from the underbrush a couple of feet off the trail. There aren't many sounds in the safe and predictable lives of modern humans that make us jump, but the hiss of a rattlesnake is one of them, triggering a dormant fear not felt regularly since the days of cave bears and saber-toothed tigers.

The third snake also rattled, but this one I saw plainly — a foot and a half away under a clump of sagebrush. Not knowing what to do, I just froze and stared at it. It was agitated, flicking the air with its tongue and twitching, as if it were ready to strike at any moment. This went on for about 20 seconds before it slowly retreated, backing away without turning its head from me. Once out of striking distance I naturally had to find a long stick to poke him with, just to see what he would do. Nothing really. Just rattle and twitch a bit more, and regret that he didn't kill me when he had the chance.

I struggle up the El Cariso Trail, a 4 x 4 road that climbs up the mountain out of Lake Elsinore. Garbage and junk strewn everywhere. Dodging moldy sofas and shattered garden furniture, I make it to the top, where the trail ends at the edge of a small pine forest. Onto the highway for a few hundred yards, stopping at a biker bar called Hell's Kitchen because I'm starving and it's my only option, wondering if any of the clientele have roared past me before, without waving, way back in the mountains of New Mexico. The patio wall is decorated with flames and skulls. Instead of advertising $1.99 burgers and happy hour specials, the sign out front features derogatory comments about our first black president and something about Muslims hating Christmas. An American flag waves out front.

I march up a one-lane road to a deserted campground, then wander around the back to locate the faint trail that leads into the canyon. This canyon is no secret, but it's seldom mentioned in hiking books because of its ruggedness and the difficulty of penetrating it after a mile or so. It's not family-friendly. If you went in with five kids you might come back out with two, and those would be snake-bitten, covered in ticks and have faces like the skin of a cantaloupe after fighting through vast thickets of poison oak. Grandma would never be seen again. The trail is not maintained and disappears altogether in places where it joins the creek bottom. In springtime, the vegetation grows completely across it. I found it many years ago by accident while wandering in circles during a lazy afternoon.

The trail begins in a meadow of brown grass and drops into a shallow depression shaded by oak trees. The gully soon deepens and an obvious streambed appears at the bottom with evidence of pools that must exist only after a hard rain. The first hour is easy going, with little elevation change and only a few sections of rock hopping across the cobbles of the dry creek. The kids would be loving it, though little Billy might get hot and tired and insist on riding up on your shoulders. Grandma might wipe her brow and clutch at her chest; don't worry, she's just winded.

The first waterfall is just up ahead, usually dry except in the wettest years, when a stream fills in and feeds the two pools below a hanging oak that sprouts from a crack in the rock. In years past the lowest branch held a hummingbird nest, no bigger than a child's teacup, the opening about the diameter of a half-dollar. I found it accidentally, by backing into it and hearing a tiny, alarmed chirp behind me. I turned around to find the nest and its irritated host staring at me from six inches away. I'd visit it on subsequent hikes and usually see a little bird sitting there or nearby, unsure if it was the same one. A couple of years ago it vanished.

The gully, a proper canyon now, drops farther and the oak trees disappear, replaced by chaparral and scattered cacti. Agave plants dot the slopes. A nearly perennial stream, only seen it dry once, flows in from a side canyon to the right, adding the sound of gurgling water to the sighing wind and chafing grass. Little Billy would insist on being let down to play in the water, where he would slip on a rock and suffer his first boo-boo.

Just downstream is the first real attraction, a 20-foot waterfall with an emerald pool below it, maybe 10 to 12 feet deep. Here the family outing would start to fall apart. Grandma would probably give up at this point, but do so heroically, saying things like, "Leave me, save yourselves," and "It's been a good life, I've had a nice run," at which point you'd leave her sitting on a boulder in a shady glade with a look of contentment on her face, watching the clouds and listening to the birds as the rest of the family soldiered on. Then you'd round a corner and she'd be gone. You'd secretly be okay with it because she was really just your mother-in-law — you only called her "Mom" because you had to — and she always was a bit of a nag.

It's possible to jump over the ledge into the pool, but your aim better be true, and how are you going to get back out if you need to? So a traverse is necessary, up to the right around a stinging yucca plant, shimmy around a hanging boulder and over a steep, gravelly slope on the other side. The twins would be frozen with fear and crying for their mommy. Little Billy would be screaming too, but only because he wanted to jump over the ledge into the pool and you wouldn't let him. There's still a path here, but if you slip there's no stopping you from sliding down the slope and flying off a 30-foot ledge to the bedrock below. I don't like heights; some people can walk right up to a thousand-foot cliff and pose confidently on the edge for a photo, while I would have to crawl up on my belly, stopping six feet short and taking their word for it that the view is incredible. So I lean into the slope and never look down, often taking a seat to slide on my butt. The last bit, about as tall as the roof of a single-story house, is vertical, but with big handholds that make it somewhat safe as long as you go easy.

The bottom holds a secret garden of hanging ferns and tufts of thick grass growing between the rocks of the stream. Alder trees, barren or with yellow leaves at this time of year, grow from the precious few spots big enough to support a trunk of their size. Cliffs rise on either side.

There's something about water that makes me want to get naked. I once spent three days on a deserted Mexican island walking around like a naked savage because I couldn't see the point in wearing clothes anymore. I've even gone surfing naked. So a hidden pool in a wild canyon is a no-brainer. I shed everything and jump in. Small snakes swim the rivulet below the pool, hunting tadpoles and yellow salamanders that live in the shallower parts of the stream. I'm hoping to God there are no leeches.

I soak in the water and sit on the rock like a naked cherub until the sun moves behind the cliff and the shaft of sunlight I'd been basking in disappears. I throw my clothes back on and set out. From here the stream enters a long, narrow chute of slickrock whose sides are studded with hundreds of tiny frogs, which cling to the rock like barnacles on a seashell. At the end of the chute the stream drops off another ledge too steep to descend.

Big problems for the family, or what's left of it. The little ones would never make it past the chute. You'd have to leave them bobbing in the pool like corks, with inflatable rings around their arms to keep their little heads above water — a bit of dog paddling wouldn't hurt them either. Timmy and Jimmy Jr., being older and in Boy Scouts, would bravely push on.

There is a way down. It's not obvious, but if you stare at it long enough it begins to reveal itself. With extreme caution it's possible to pick a path down the 70-degree slope to the bottom, where a fallen tree crosses the deep pool below. Two minutes farther is another waterfall, this one higher than the first two and overhanging. A frayed nylon rope tied around a boulder vanishes over the ledge. It has loops in it at intervals, but it's so old and brittle-looking I'm not willing to chance it. A second traverse is required, no trail at all this time, with loose rock underfoot and few handholds. After 45 minutes of studying the route and second-guessing, I pick my way down, the whole time thinking, "Thank God I don't have to come back this way."

By now the family would be done-for. Jimmy Jr., being an Eagle Scout whose favorite merit badge was in knot-tying, would decide to try the frayed rope off the side of the last waterfall, convinced it was all in the way you knotted it. And that would be that. Timmy you would have thrown off the cliff yourself because you caught him raiding the picnic basket.

Another waterfall, then another. No trail, no sign of anyone being here in a very long time. It's hard to believe a canyon this deep, dramatic and pristine lies just a few miles from millions of people.

A third or fourth traverse, I'm losing track. This one is bad, with loose rock on a slope with nearly impenetrable brush, and the hill so steep it's hard not to call it a cliff. I'm no longer sure which types of plants I'm smashing through, and up until now I've been studiously avoiding anything that looks like poison oak. This plant, the bane of my existence on previous hikes, is generally identifiable by its three-leaf clusters — "Leaves of three, let it be" as the Scouts would have said, were they still around to say it. It's often at its worst late in the season when the leaves turn purple or even bright red. Already in this canyon I have seen large patches of it, recognizable only by a few scraggly leaves still hanging in a forest of bare stems.

What I don't realize at this time is that the stems, and not just the leaves, are capable of causing the allergic skin reaction this plant is famous for. In about a week the entire surfaces of both legs, both arms and most of my back will be covered in puffy, oozing red sores. When I go to the doctor, her first reaction will be, "Oh my God!" Then one after another her curious colleagues will wander in to gawk at me and say unhelpful things like "Eww!", "Ouch!" and "That doesn't look like fun!" Only a shot of Benadryl and cortisone followed by a five-day course of steroids will knock it out, and this after ten days of misery.

Back on my hillside, or cliff, or whatever you want to call it, the going is rough. I'm barely moving, trying to break through the brush while still watching where my feet land so I don't step on any snakes, though I think it unlikely they'd be on an incline as steep as this. The only good thing about these stabbing, slashing bushes is that they give me something to hold onto as I try not to slide off the sheer wall. I hump over a ridge and come to a ledge, about shoulder-width and 10 feet long, with a large cliff below it. At the far end of the ledge is a vertical climb of 15 feet to what looks like a manageable slope.

I look over my shoulder and the way I came suddenly looks impossible. Did I really climb over that? For the first time I think this might be a bad idea, a very bad idea. But, spurred on by adrenaline and stupidity — a lethal combination — I keep going, convinced I still know what I'm doing. This is debatable, and becomes more so as I shuffle across the ledge and stare up at the vertical wall to the slope above. There are definite handholds, but as I climb up the pack is pulling me backward, off the rock face, and I can't help fixating on each placement of my hands and feet, realizing that if I slip or one of my handholds gives way, I'm dead. I stop for a few seconds to survey, but all I can think is, "You are such a moron . . . you are such a moron . . . no, really, you're a moron."

There have been three times when I was well and truly in fear for my life. Once in a jetliner, taking off into a sudden storm front pushing in from the ocean, during which the plane rattled and dove to the extent that luggage was flying around in the cabin, everyone was screaming and barfing and the wings seemed to flex 10 feet in either direction; a second time, on a poorly planned mountaineering expedition, when I passed out at the foot of a glacier from altitude sickness and had to be carried semi-conscious down the mountain by porters; and a third time while surfing, when a Great White shark appeared in the lineup and everyone cleared out before I knew what was happening, leaving me out there by myself.

This moment will rank with the others, if I survive it. I will either die in this canyon, with my remains scattered by coyotes and bobcats, or I will appear on the 8 o'clock news as the guy dangling from a basket beneath the chopper while, watching from home, Del says to Doris: "Great. Another idiot endangering the lives of our rescue guys and wasting my taxpayer dollars trying to drag his sorry butt out of there. Hope they charge him for it . . ."

This isn't helping. I'm sweating; my fingers are wet and slippery. The last knob of rock before making the slope above is not a good one, no real lip to curl my fingers over, just an angled, lichen-covered spot on which two fingers might hold, or they might slip right off. I always wanted to be reincarnated as a dolphin. Now is my chance.

I grope the rock with my fingers, then lean into it. My fingers hold. I make it. Thank you, God. It's still sketchy, but the brush is once again so thick it's nearly impossible to fall, because it's nearly impossible to move through it. I struggle 10 feet in five minutes. At the bottom I break through the last section, as thick as a hedgerow, and fall blindly forward into the creek.

I'm soaked up to my chest. It's getting late, and it's been over four hours since I saw a spot big and flat enough to lie down in. Until now I had been taking off my shoes every time I came to a pool, then putting them back on once I waded across. It no longer matters. I just jump right in, shoes and clothes be damned, my only concern being my sleeping bag, which will not keep me warm if it gets wet. But wet shoes mean the very real possibility of slipping on rocks and hitting my head or breaking bones. A couple of times I do slide and my feet completely come out from under me, like I've just been thrown by a wrestler, but both times I land on my back and the pack cushions my fall. Lucky. I crawl around room-sized boulders and tree trunks, expecting the canyon to open up just around the next corner, pleading for it to do so before the sun goes down.

Lighter up ahead. The canyon is opening up. Salvation. But something is not right. The stream drops in several steps, into deep pools that trickle over the edges into other pools, until there is one final ledge. I can see the creek skip playfully up and over that last lip of rock, but there is no sound afterward, no splashing as the water hits the bottom. The wind is blowing the plume back up and over itself. It's leaping into open air, into space, into nothing.

I scramble up a shoulder of rock to my right, and . . . I see nothing. I can't see the bottom. The rock slopes sharply to a drop off, and I'm too frightened to get closer. But I know it's bad. I'm guessing it's at least 150 feet, maybe 200, to the bottom. And just then I realize my mistake. Somehow, perhaps from the fog of too little sleep or the excitement of embarking on this one final adventure, I'd forgotten a critical detail — that this canyon is home to the highest waterfall in the Santa Ana Mountains, a drop of 170 feet. For a brief moment I consider the mother of all traverses, but no, certain death, nearly vertical canyon walls and crumbling rock. And the sun is just setting.

I want to cry but I'm too tired. So I just plop down on the rock with my head in my hands. "You are such a moron . . ."

The sun is gone. The canyon is dark. Wind coming up, temperature dropping. Pull it together. I stand up and realize I've just been granted two strokes of luck. The first involved not making the move I almost made, which would have been sliding over the second-to-last slope of rock to peek right over the final precipice. From this angle I can see it would have been very difficult, maybe impossible, to get back up out of there, with slick, wet rock and no handholds. I might have been trapped between that slope and a 170-foot drop-off. Possibly my final blunder. The second bit of luck is at my feet, where I find the only flat spot I've seen since entering the canyon, a rock ledge just big enough to lie down on, a little island bordered by the stream and two pools. The cliff is 20 feet away. This is it for the night.

The wind is swirling, changing direction every few seconds. I throw rocks inside the tent to keep it from blowing off the cliff and drifting away like a hot air balloon with no hot air inside. I'm becoming paranoid about mountain lions again, though the chances of attack are so slim it should be the least of my worries. The situation is heightening my fear. I'm seeing ghosts in the trees and monsters in the pools. And mountain lions in every crevice.

Mountain lions? They do like to hunt at night. Check. They also like to leap down on unsuspecting prey from higher spots like the ledge directly over my head. Check. And whenever I bend down to settle the tent or get something out of my pack, I'm just about the same height and shape as a small deer. Checkmate?

I eat my Spaghettios and submerge the can in the water under a rock to hide the scent. It always works in the movies. I'll fish it out in the morning.

A beautiful spot. The canyon is deep, many hundreds of feet below the surrounding ridges. The pools all around glow orange in the twilight. The alder growing in the crevice above creaks in the wind, its few remaining leaves fluttering down upon my head with the strongest gusts. Drifting clouds blaze red on top like an armada of ships with their sails on fire, retreating before a stronger enemy. Far in the distance, for the first time, I can see the shimmering Pacific. I will see it again.

Lie down, exhale, sleep.

At daybreak I'm on my way. The ledge looks no less deadly, the canyon no less intimidating in the new light of dawn. I didn't sleep much as the wind picked up during the night. With no way to tie down the sides of the tent on the barren rock, they just collapsed around my head whenever the wind blew, like someone trying to suffocate me with Saran Wrap. I pack up, toss a few rocks in the pool, and leave.

Exhausted after an hour and I can't afford to be. The first traverse. I go up a different way, getting torn up by the brush. I turn sideways, then nearly backwards, using my pack to bust a path like an ice breaker. I'm no longer worried about snakes. Too tired to care. My legs are a bloody mess, as if someone took a cheese grater to them or they were attacked by hungry hamsters. Small flies are landing on the wounds. I get to a place I didn't come through, a very dangerous place. Navigating blindly, only certain of the cliff a few feet away and the general direction I need to be heading. I finally make it to a spot I recognize, the dangerous vertical drop with the ledge beneath and the cliff beyond that. Everything looks different from this angle, in fact it looks impossible though I know I came up this way. I look up and for a few brief seconds I consider climbing up the slope and out onto the ridge above, but I have no idea how far away it is, maybe a mile or farther, and at this rate I wouldn't make it in an entire day of smashing and crashing through the underbrush. And if I need to be rescued, a real possibility at this point, they won't find me in the dense vegetation of the slope unless I start a fire and burn the whole thing down with me in it. So my choices are to continue sitting here, hoping someone finds me after a few days when I don't show up and someone calls the authorities, or continuing up the way I came yesterday. I weigh the options. I'll be out of water and food in another day, and I can't cling to this hillside for three or four days. If I fall asleep, which I would do eventually, I'd roll off the side and over the cliff.

So I choose the ledge. I'm not swinging over the side with a 40-pound pack on my back, so I take it off and prepare to chuck it at the ledge below. If I miss and it goes over the cliff I can still make it to the road by sundown, only out six or seven hundred dollars' worth of gear. Do I care at this point? Aim and let it drop. It bounces a couple of times and settles on the ledge. I inch my way down, certain death a finger slip away. But without the pack it's makeable.

The other traverses are progressively easier, but I'm totally exhausted. My legs are shaking. I wiggle around the rock above the last pool, and I know I've made it. Happy, so happy. I look down at the water and the kids we'd left bobbing in the pool yesterday are nowhere to be found. Little Billy probably got carried off to be raised in a cave by coyotes. He always was a wild one. The wife is not going to be happy when you get home.

But that's your problem, not mine. I was only trying to kill myself, not my entire family. I make it to the campground in the afternoon and collapse on a picnic table, grateful to have survived one of the dumbest things I've ever done. I still have the highway to contend with, which I'm not willing to do after just cheating death in the wild. I locate the San Juan Trail, which follows the top of the ridge south of the canyon, and stumble down. At dusk I'm at the mouth of the canyon, at the car park at trail's end, with a paved road leading out. The return of "No Trespassing" signs but I don't care. In the dark I find a gate I can squeeze through, boulder hop across the stream, and sleep in a beautiful, lush meadow thick with grass and overhanging trees.

HOME

Halfway down the trail I crossed into Orange County. Shiny, glittery Orange County. Home to the West Coast's largest pleasure boat harbor and America's number one Mercedes-Benz dealership. Cradle of civilization to wealthy Republicans. My home.

At a 7-Eleven a lowered SUV with spinning rims pulls into the crowded parking lot and straddles the line between parking spots, thereby taking up two of them. Three shirtless guys with tattoos and nascent beer guts pile out and walk down the street, shorts pulled down below their underwear, belts pulled tight like tourniquets around the middle of their thighs. Inside the store, some sort of petrified, ultra-processed food items — the sign says "Taquitos de pollo con queso Monterrey Jack" — are spinning hypnotically beneath a heat lamp. I'm trying to guess how many days they've been there when a group of young women pushes to the front and shovels the entire inventory into several paper bags. They're wearing an incredible amount of makeup. Spray tan and layers of foundation have turned their skin orange, and I realize they don't have any eyebrows — they've been completely plucked off and drawn back on with a pencil. They look like Oompa Loompas from *Willy Wonka and the Chocolate Factory*. Back in New Mexico I watched a woman walk into a diner dressed in dirty jeans and chaps, bandana around her neck, cowboy hat in hand. Twigs in her hair and boots that smelled like horse shit. A cowgirl, working. And she was stunning. So much so that I broke my three-second rule by about three seconds. Now I'm surrounded by women who wouldn't be caught dead outside with real eyebrows.

I walk past Mission San Juan Capistrano, built in 1776 when there was virtually no other European habitation on the coast of California. Now it's lost in a sea of commercial development and housing tracts. Stop at the library to use the facilities and a man outside says hello.

"Where you walking from?"

"Maine."

"Oh."

I guess he didn't understand me, or he thinks I'm coming from Main Street, or he meets people walking from Maine every day.

Into Dana Point. There's the Pacific. Right there. All I have to do is walk across the street and dip my big toe in it, and this journey is over. But I'm going home, to the exact spot where I learned how to surf and love the ocean. Just a little farther.

The wind is blowing hard out of the north, piling huge drifts of leaves on the sidewalks where the lawn meets the pavement. After a quick check for lurking gardeners, I kick through the piles, scattering leaves in the street and flower beds. And if it was raining I'd be stomping in the flooded gutters with my shoes on. When I'm 97 years old I hope I'm still doing it.

Past the Montage, a beach resort where room prices start at $1,100 a night on a weekend in summer and shoot up from there. I once found a $20 bill in a tide pool out front. Mansions line the cliffs — $10 million homes and up not unusual here. Several years ago a house just up the coast was listed at $75 million.

In my former life as a news photographer I once shot a home tour here, an event in which people open their homes to common folk for a day so they can ooh and ahh at the incredible architecture and fuss over all the nice stuff they have. In the entryway of the first house a painting hung on the wall. Looked old. A docent walked up to me, gushing.

"Isn't it magnificent?"

"Yeah, that's nice. Looks real."

"It *is* real," she said, slightly put off.

"What is it?"

"It's a Rembrandt."

I pondered it for a second, swimming in a fantasy that began with "smash and grab" and ended with piña coladas on the beach in Cabo. The docent was still staring at me, waiting for a reaction.

"Shouldn't that thing be in a museum?"

She made a sniffing noise and walked away to find someone more appreciative of having a priceless artwork hanging in the doorway of some guy's house. I finished taking pictures of the infinity pool with the stunning ocean view and walked out the door thinking about the 40% of the world's population that lives on less than two dollars a day. Yeah, I know. I'm a party-pooper.

DAY 175

I'm thinking of stingrays as I sprint across the sandbar, sunlight rippling across the bottom through the cold water. My shoes are on the beach, my 13th pair, along with 30 or so good people who came out to cheer, make some hamburgers and hot dogs, hang a couple of signs in my honor. Good people. The kind I met in Kansas. The kind I live with.

With a final lurch I flop into the sea. I don't know what to feel. This was the journey that was going to change everything, the time when I was going to figure everything out. None of that happened. But I'm unconcerned. In this one moment I'm a little less worried that I never followed the blueprint to live my life, that I've paid dearly in comfort and security to have experiences most people will only dream of having. I've seen the Northern Lights, and the southern. I've stood on glaciers at the equator. Touched the skin of a whale. Sat in a meadow with a family of gorillas on the flank of a volcano. And I have walked across America. I'm grateful for every day that I'm alive. And when people ask me if I found what I was looking for I will say: No, I did not. I had an adventure.

I stand in the ocean a long time. I've found my water again. The Pacific is calm and smooth. Dolphins are playing in the waves; in another life I'll be one of them. I trace the blue arc of the sky overhead, and back the way I came, across the desert, the mountains, the places where the corn rustles at night and the sand blows across the road in ribbons, and all the lost and lonely miles.

Made in the USA
Columbia, SC
02 September 2020